TOM BRADY

THE GOAT

Everyone has an opinion on who the greatest NFL player of all time is. But there's a reason why many people from New England, across America, and all over the world mention Tom Brady.

Tom Brady is often called the greatest NFL player of all time because of where he started out, and the work he put in to become the legend that he is today. He was the face of the Patriots dynasty for 20 years and he's been named NFL MVP three times and won seven Super Bowl rings.

Brady started out with a solid college football career at the University of Michigan from 1995–1999, and an

amazing final game, where he threw five touchdowns and led the Wolverines to an upset win over Alabama in the Orange Bowl. But his path to superstardom wasn't guaranteed. While many superstars are often drafted very high (within the first two rounds of the yearly NFL Draft), Tom Brady was selected 199th overall once he left Michigan. He was a lowly sixth-round pick.

Most sixth- or seventh-round picks are lucky to even make a team's practice squad. Most of them are cut after preseason games in the summer when teams are trying to get their rosters down to 53 players. But not only was Tom Brady drafted very low, but his predraft workout was also extremely average.

He had an extremely unimpressive workout, including an extremely slow 40-yard dash. Most NFL prospects run the 40 in under 4.8 seconds, even big offensive and defensive linemen. Brady ran his at a snail's pace—5.28 seconds. This led him to tumble way down the draft board, but it also led to several people writing him off. The negative comments from scouts were everywhere.

"Lacks great physical stature and strength."

"Lacks mobility."

"Does not throw a very tight spiral."

"A system-type player who can get exposed, and is forced to improvise."

Tom Brady felt hurt that teams weren't giving him the respect he deserved. "It was hard. I remember taking a walk with my mom and dad around the block. It was just a tough day. They took it as emotionally as I do," he said.

But instead of being bitter and letting his disappointment ruin him, he used it as a chip on his shoulder

TRULY INSPIRATIONAL
FOOTBALL
STORIES
FOR YOUNG READERS

250 FUN SPORTS FACTS INCLUDED

ETHAN WILSON

TABLE OF CONTENTS

CONTENTS		2
1.	**Tom Brady:** The GOAT	3
2.	**Baker Mayfield:** From Walk-on to NFL Sta	11
3.	**Doug Flutie:** Overcoming the Odds	19
4.	**Vince Papale:** Mr. Invincible	28
5.	**Detroit Lions:** Restoring the Roar!	36
6.	**The Cleveland Summit:** Bravery in Action	44
7.	**Gale Sayers and Brian Piccolo:** An Unlikely Friendship	52
8.	**Walter Payton:** A Lesson in Selflessness from Sweetness	60
9.	**Pat Tillman:** Passion and Patriotism	68
10.	**Derrick Thomas:** Kansas City's Gentle Giant	76
11.	**Brett Favre:** #4 Wins One for His Dad	85
12.	**Kurt Warner:** Faith Through Adversity	93
13.	**CJ Stroud:** Faith and Football	101
14.	**Michael Irvin:** Keeping the Promise	109
15.	**Josh Jacobs:** From Rags to Riches	117
16.	**2009 New Orleans Saints:** Winning after Tragedy	125
17.	**Joe Thomas:** Mr. Consistency	133
18.	**1993 AFC Wild Card Game:** Greatest Comeback in NFL History	141
19.	**Denver Broncos:** Galloping toward Glory with John Elway	149
20.	**Jerry Rice:** The GOAT of Wide Receivers!	157
	References	165

to drive him to bigger and better things. A comment he made to Patriots owner Robert Kraft was just a glimpse of the fire that was burning inside him.

"I'm the best decision this franchise has ever made," he declared. He was eager to prove everyone wrong, and wasn't afraid to let his new boss know that he would do whatever it took to win.

Brady started his career fourth on the Patriots depth chart in 2000. Most NFL teams only have three quarterbacks on their rosters. Brady's competitive fire was only stoked by that perceived snub. And it wouldn't be long before he got the chance to show what he could do, as the Pats' quarterback of the future.

After Patriots starting quarterback Drew Bledsoe went down with a concussion in the second game of the 2001 season, 24-year-old Tom Brady took over. He started 14 games that season. The Patriots went 11-3, while Brady threw for over 2,800 yards, 18 touchdowns, and 12 interceptions.

Bledsoe recovered later on, and appeared a couple of times in the playoffs. But Tom Brady led New England to wins over the Oakland Raiders and Pittsburgh Steelers to help the Patriots advance to Super Bowl 36, their third Super Bowl appearance in team history at the time.

But even though the Pats made their first Super Bowl appearance since 1996, they had yet to win a Championship, and were heavy underdogs to a team nicknamed "the Greatest Show on Turf," the St. Louis Rams.

The odds were stacked firmly against New England. But like their young leader Tom Brady, the Patriots weren't intimidated. They believed in themselves. They were fearless. They used the negativity surrounding them as fuel.

After all, they were two touchdown underdogs, and were expected to get blown out.

Tom Brady had been doubted ever since he came into the league, and the Patriots had been laughed at and disrespected, as a team just lucky to be there. But how they played in Super Bowl 36 would wipe the smug smirk off the face of every hater.

The stout Patriots defense shut down the Rams high-powered offensive attack. New England played so well that they held a 17-3 lead going into the fourth quarter. But the Rams broke free, and struck back with two touchdowns to tie the game at 17. That left just 90 seconds for the Patriots to put together a game-winning drive. The spotlight was now on Tom Brady, in the biggest moment of his young life. Thirty-one other NFL teams wrote him off. They didn't want him, they disrespected him, and he was about to make them all regret that mistake.

Brady completed five of his six passes on the final drive of the game, and drove the Patriots offense all the way down to the Rams 30-yard line, and spiked the ball with seven seconds left. This set up Adam Vinatieri for the game-winning field goal. The veteran kicker, who had never missed a kick indoors, drilled it from 47 yards out without a second thought. Pats win, 20-17.

Just like that, the Patriots were on top of the football world. And their unlikely hero had achieved something most people can only fantasize about in their wildest dreams. He was now a World Champion and Super Bowl MVP at just 24 years old.

From there, Tom Brady's career took off. Over the course of the next two decades, he would lead new England to victories in Super Bowl 38 (2003 season), Super Bowl 39 (2004 season), Super Bowl 49 (2014 season), Super Bowl

51 (2016 season), and Super Bowl 53 (2018 season). He also led the Tampa Bay Buccaneers to a Championship with a win over the Kansas City Chiefs in Super Bowl 55 (2020 season), before finally hanging up his cleats for good at 43 years old.

He was also named Super Bowl MVP five times in his career, and will be a first-ballot Hall of Famer in 2028. But it all began when he was drafted 199th overall. A player who was lucky to even make the Patriots' roster, ended up becoming the greatest player of all time.

Tom Brady had a stubborn work ethic. He refused to quit. He didn't listen to the negative voices in his head, or the haters who doubted him and made fun of him. And he put together one of the greatest legacies in sports history!

You may or may not end up being a superstar football player like him. And that's completely okay. But whether you choose to pursue athletic dreams, or you decide to become a doctor, lawyer, firefighter, police officer, or anything else, Tom Brady's story can still serve as an inspiration for you.

The desire to do something you're passionate about, coupled with hard work, can produce amazing results. And this can be true whether you have a natural talent for something, or if you have to work extremely hard to get good at it.

Tom Brady may be a seven-time World Champion, five-time Super Bowl MVP, three-time NFL MVP, and the greatest quarterback in history. But at the end of the day, he's something even more simple: a normal man who never gave up.

Take a cue from the GOAT: Never give up on your dreams, no matter what they may be!

- He didn't train like a typical athlete or football player. While most football players lift weights, Tom Brady focused on using resistance bands to increase his flexibility. He believed that long, soft muscles would help him perform better.

- He sacrificed over $100 Million he could have made, and instead allowed the Patriots to use that money to sign better players to help the team compete for, and win Super Bowls.

- Tom Brady felt so well prepared, that he fell asleep before his first Super Bowl against the Rams in 2001. Luckily, he woke up with 12 minutes to spare, led the Patriots out onto the field, and the rest is history.

- To keep his mind sharp during his playing career, he used brain exercises that are normally reserved for people struggling with the effects of brain injuries, such as memory loss.

- Seven-time Super Bowl Champion. That's a record!

- Tom Brady grew up a 49ers fan.

- The Patriots were planning on building their future around Drew Bledsoe. He had just signed a big contract extension. But when he went down with an injury early in the 2001 season, Tom Brady took over and never looked back!

- Led New England to the first 16-0 regular season in NFL history in 2007.

- Was married to supermodel Gisele Bundchen from 2009 to 2022.

- As of this book, Tom Brady is currently retired. But he has suggested coming out of retirement to continue playing at nearly 47 years old!

1. Where did Tom Brady play college football?

2. True or false: Tim Brady is in the Hall of Fame.

3. How many times has Tom Brady made the Pro Bowl?

4. How many times has Tom Brady led the league in passing touchdowns?

5. How many wins does Tom Brady have in his career?

6. How many games has Tom Brady won in the Playoffs?

7. How many career passing touchdowns does Tom Brady have?

8. True or false: Tom Brady is on the NFL 100th Anniversary Team.

9. True or False: Tom Brady has never lost in the Super Bowl.

10. True or false: Tom Brady is set to be a color commentator for the 2024 season.

ANSWER

1. *The University of Michigan.*
2. *False, but if five years has gone by and he's still retired, he's a guaranteed first-ballot Hall of Famer!*
3. *15 times.*
4. *Five times.*
5. *251 wins as a starting quarterback, an NFL record.*
6. *35 times, an NFL record.*
7. *649, an NFL record.*
8. *True!*
9. *False. He's lost in the Super Bowl three times, twice to Eli Manning and the New York Giants.*
10. *True!*

"I think sometimes in life the biggest challenges end up being the best things that happen in your life."

"If you don't play to win don't play at all."

"Too often in life, something happens and we blame other people for us not being happy or satisfied or fulfilled. So the point is, we all have choices, and we make the choice to accept people or situations or to not accept situations."

"A lot of times I find that people who are blessed with the most talent don't ever develop that attitude, and the ones who aren't blessed in that way are the most competitive and have the biggest heart."

"I'm not a person who defends myself very often. I kind of let my actions speak for me."

LESSONS FROM THE STORY

- Don't listen to the haters. Just do the best you can do with what you have.

- Have confidence in yourself!

- Leaders step up and take charge when no one else will.

- Be the best teammate, person and friend that you can be

- A great work ethic can cover up a lot of weaknesses.

BAKER MAYFIELD

FROM WALK-ON TO NFL STAR

While the subject of this story is now one of the NFL's stars, his road to success wasn't easy. It was bumpy, and filled with all kinds of obstacles and detours. But if you know who Baker Mayfield is, he likes it that way. The Buccaneers' starting quarterback is considered short for his position at 6'1", and slightly undersized at 215 pounds. But he's used these shortcomings, as well as everything negative that's ever been said about him, as fuel on his journey.

This competitive fire first started showing up long before he ever took a snap in the NFL. Baker was originally a three-star recruit coming out of Lake Travis High School, Texas. While he did get a few offers from smaller NCAA schools, Mayfield didn't get any scholarship offers from any major colleges; he instead opted to walk on at Texas Tech, a big-time college in the Big 12 Conference.

For a while, Mayfield lit it up as a Red Raider. In seven starts for the team, he won five of those games, threw for over 2,300 yards, and 12 touchdowns. But after he suffered a knee injury in the middle of the season, he was forced to sit out three games. Things got weird then.

After Mayfield healed up enough to play, his coach at the time, Kliff Kingsbury still wouldn't play him for some reason. Texas Tech also never offered him a scholarship, even though he had been solid in his time with the team. So Baker decided to transfer to Oklahoma to play football for the Sooners, the team he rooted for as a boy growing up in Texas. His first meeting with head coach Bob Stoops would also show glimpses of the player he would become.

While most players would contact a coach by phone, or another formal way to announce their desire to play for the team, Baker took it a step further. He had the confidence to walk right into the room where the coaching staff was eating dinner that night, and he introduced himself to Stoops, a famous football coach, in person.

After sitting out the 2014 season because of transferring, Baker entered 2015 excited, amped up, and ready to show the world what he could do! Mayfield had one of the best seasons of his life in 2015, leading Oklahoma to an 11-2 record, throwing for over 3,700 yards, 36 touchdowns, and 7 interceptions. He even led the Sooners to the College Football Playoff, which gave them a chance to compete for the National Championship! Not only that, but his statistics were also good enough to push him to national recognition.

As a 20-year-old Sophomore, he finished fourth in the voting for the Heisman Trophy, which is awarded to the best college football player in the country. The undersized kid from

Austin, Texas, who had always wanted to play football for his favorite team growing up, was now doing just that. And not only was he winning, the team was getting better and better under his leadership as well. He was on an upward climb and so were the Sooners!

The year 2016 was another solid one for Baker Mayfield and Oklahoma. He threw for over 3,900 yards and 40 touchdowns, while leading the Sooners to another 11-2 record. But the highlight of the season wasn't a rivalry win against Texas. And it wasn't a win over Auburn to end the year. The highlight of the 2016 season for Baker Mayfield came on October 22, 2016, against his old team—the Texas Tech.

High-scoring football games are often called shootouts. But this one wasn't just a shootout. It was a straight-up fireworks show. Oklahoma and Texas Tech put up a final score that looked more like something you'd see after a college basketball game instead of a football game!

But it wasn't just an instant classic for the ages. The game featured Baker Mayfield at his absolute best, along with another NFL great—future Hall of Famer Patrick Mahomes. Mahomes and Mayfield dueled with each other in one of the most entertaining battles of all time!

The two combined to throw for 12 touchdowns and over 1,200 yards. Oklahoma won the game 66-59 behind Baker Mayfield's 7 touchdowns and 545 yards. But Patrick Mahomes had the better individual game, throwing for an insane 734 yards and 5 touchdowns, while also adding two rushing touchdowns. But Baker Mayfield not only got the last word in a huge battle for the ages, he also got the last laugh with Texas Tech head coach Kliff Kingsbury, who had decided to not give him a scholarship, or let him be the starter two years earlier.

This game would be Mayfield's coming out party. But it was a springboard for even bigger things moving forward. Not only was he named the Heisman Trophy Winner in 2017, but he was also drafted number one overall by the Cleveland Browns the next year. It seemed like the perfect pairing. The natural-born underdog was going to a city that was starved for a winner. Cleveland is a city full of blue-collar people who work hard for everything they get. Baker would embody that mindset for the first four years of his career.

His time in Cleveland was a roller coaster. In 2018, the brash young rookie helped the Browns snap a skid where they won only one game in two years, as he led the Browns to seven wins. But in 2019 he took a step back, and the team did too as Cleveland fell to 6-10.

But his best year as a Brown came in 2020. Not only did he lead the team to an 11-5 record, their highest win total since 1994, he also led them to their first playoff win since January 1995 when they beat the Steelers in the AFC Wild Card Game. But a tough injury would sadly spell the end of his time in Cleveland, and would lead to another downswing in his life and career.

A torn labrum in his shoulder from an injury suffered during the next season would eventually lead to him being traded away from Cleveland, and he bounced around the league, playing for both the Panthers and Rams before landing in Tampa Bay with the Buccaneers. Before he landed in Tampa as a free agent, people were ready to write him off. He was awful in his short time as a starter for the Panthers, and he was merely a placeholder for the Rams as they finished a bad season. He was staring at the very realistic possibility of being a backup quarterback for the rest of his career.

But as Baker had done so many times before, he decided he was going to continue fighting. He wasn't going to listen to the doubters and haters; he wasn't finished yet. He'd have to make his comeback with the team that had just been led by the greatest quarterback of all time—Tom Brady. Those were massive shoes to fill. But if anyone had the confidence to rise to that kind of challenge, Baker did.

He would do just that, as he would win nine games as a starter, and throw for over 4,000 yards and 28 touchdowns (both career highs). And he would also win the second playoff game of his career by leading the Bucs to a blowout win over the Philadelphia Eagles. And even though he lost the next week to the Detroit Lions, it was clear: Baker was back!

From the lows of being snubbed by Texas Tech and being traded away from the Browns, to the highs of being the first walk-on player to ever win the Heisman Trophy, and leading Cleveland and Tampa Bay to playoff victories, Baker Mayfield has weathered the storms of his life and career by having a confident belief in himself, working hard, and being patient. If you've ever been discouraged by someone to chase after your dreams, but you know you have the skills and belief to make them happen? Don't take no for an answer.

If you're not as talented as other people at something you love to do? That's okay. Continue to practice and work hard, and the dream will become a reality.

Baker Mayfield was seen as small, and not quite as talented as some of his rival quarterbacks in college and the pros. Teams passed on the opportunity to have him play for them. But now he's a starting quarterback entering his seventh season in the NFL in 2024 because he never gave up. He bet on himself both in life and football.

If you do the same, and put in the hard work to get where you want to be, the only person who can stop you is yourself. Take a lesson from #6 himself: "It doesn't matter what cards you're dealt. It's what you do with those cards. Never complain. Just keep pushing forward. Find a positive in anything and just fight for it."

- Baseball was his first love when it came to sports. He played in the infield growing up, but his main positions were shortstop and third base.

- Baker had a massive growth spurt in high school. As a freshman he was really short at 5'2. But by his junior year he was almost 5'10.

- Baker is a huge fan of Seinfeld and The Walking Dead.

- Went #1 overall in 2018 to the Cleveland Browns.

- Guided the Browns to their first playoff win in 26 years in January 2020, when they knocked off their hated rival, the Pittsburgh Steelers.

- Made his first career Pro Bowl appearance in 2023.

- Led the Rams on a 98-yard game-winning touchdown drive after being claimed by them the same week!

- Grew up as a fan of the Oklahoma Sooners, despite being from Texas.

- Played for the Sooners from 2014 to 2017.

- Won the Heisman Trophy in 2017 as the best player in America!

1. True or false: Baker Mayfield was a 5-star recruit in high school.

2. True or false: He was immediately awarded the starting quarterback job for Oklahoma.

3. True or false: Baker won Rookie of the Year with the Browns in 2018.

4. How many siblings does Baker Mayfield have?

5. True or False: He predicted that he would one day play in the NFL.

6. True or false: Baker beat Chiefs legend Patrick Mahomes in one of the greatest college football games in history.

7. True or false: Baker Mayfield's dad, James Mayfield, also played college football when he was younger.

8. How many touchdown passes did Baker throw during his rookie season in Cleveland in 2018?

9. True or False: Baker currently has over 20,000 passing yards.

10. True or False: Baker threw for four touchdowns in the first half of an NFL game.

ANSWER

1. *False. He was a three-star recruit, which made him work that much harder.*
2. *False. He walked onto the team, and climbed his way up the depth chart.*
3. *False. Saquon Barkley of the Giants won Rookie of the Year, but Baker was named to the All-Rookie Team.*
4. *He has one older brother, Matt Mayfield, who was a standout baseball player in college at Texas A&M.*
5. *True! He predicted in the sixth grade that he would one day play in the NFL.*
6. *True! Baker went off in that game in 2016 for Oklahoma, throwing for 545 yards and seven touchdowns! The Sooners won 66-59!*
7. *True! He played for the Houston Cougars.*
8. *27, which was a rookie record at the time.*
9. *True! He currently has an impressive 20,332 passing yards, as he goes into his seventh season in the NFL.*
10. *True! He threw for four touchdowns in the first half of a game vs. the Titans in 2020, which helped the Browns ultimately earn their first winning season in 13 years!*

QUOTES

"It doesn't matter what cards you're dealt. It's what you do with those cards. Never complain. Just keep pushing forward. Find a positive in anything and just fight for it."

"Family first, always, no matter what the situation."

"I've set up my goals, and I go after them, and if I do that each day, the rest will take care of itself."

"When people doubt me, I want to prove them wrong."

"Not everybody responds to yelling at 'em or jumping all over 'em. Sometimes you need to put your arm around somebody and encourage them."

LESSONS FROM THE STORY

- Don't listen to the outside noise. Just do the best you can do.

- Have confidence in your abilities, but stay humble. There's always more to learn.

- Often you have to go through adversity in life to ultimately be who you eventually become.

- The only person who can stop you from achieving your dreams, is yourself.

- If you want something bad enough, keep working for it. Don't take no for an answer.

3

DOUG FLUTIE

OVERCOMING THE ODDS

A few shorter quarterbacks have now made their mark in the NFL, such as Drew Brees, Russell Wilson, and Baker Mayfield. But perhaps the first one to open the door for them, and really make some noise, was Doug Flutie.

At 5'9" and 175 pounds, Flutie was considered too small to play any level of football. But over the course of his time playing football in college, the NFL, and the Canadian Football League, Flutie has become arguably the greatest sports example of why you should never judge a book by its cover. Or why you should always give someone a chance to prove what they can do before counting them out.

A "perfect" NFL-ready quarterback typically stands at least 6'3", weighs at least 220 pounds, and has a rocket arm. Doug Flutie didn't have any of those qualities. But his heart, stubborn refusal to give up, and his never say die attitude silenced a lot of haters. But he would have to endure a lot of disrespect both as a kid and grown man before taking his place as one of the greatest football players of all time.

When his parents found him sleeping holding a football at four years old, it didn't matter what kind of obstacles Flutie would face in his life. He loved the game of football, and would give his all to the sport. He was destined to be a football player, no matter what it took.

His first obstacle that he would have to overcome was a big one. As a freshman at Boston College, the only school to offer him a scholarship, Flutie wasn't the second or third string quarterback. He was all the way down at #9 on the depth chart at quarterback. Yes, he was the ninth quarterback on the depth chart. But he kept his head down, worked hard, and eventually made his way into a game against Penn State late in the season.

The Boston College Eagles were getting pulverized by Penn State 38-0 when the coach finally gave Flutie his chance to come into the game. Flutie would only manage to throw one touchdown pass in a lopsided win for Penn State, but he showed off his elusiveness and ability to sling the football.

This impressed the head coach enough to make Flutie the full-time starter from that point on. And Flutie handled himself like a seasoned veteran. He wasn't cocky, but he was definitely confident in his abilities as a quarterback, even though he only stood at 5'9" and weighed just 175 pounds.

In an interview with NFL Network for the film *Doug Flutie: A Football Life*, Flutie said that throwing the football in his college debut was just like playing pickup football with his older brother Bill and their friends.

"All these guys were telling me I was too short and how complicated the game is. But it was not that complicated. It was the same game I always played."

Over the next three seasons, Flutie would use that confidence and his skills to carve out a reputation for himself as the most exciting player in college football. Whether it was throwing long bombs for touchdowns, scrambling for first downs, or improvising and throwing the football on the run, Flutie could do it all. He finished third in the Heisman Trophy voting his junior season in 1983. But it's what would happen on November 23, 1984, that would launch Doug Flutie to Heisman-winning glory and college football immortality.

The "55 Flood Tip." That was the name of the play. Defending National Champion Miami was the opponent. It was a true David vs. Goliath matchup. The game was a straight up shootout, with Miami Hurricanes quarterback Bernie Kosar throwing for a school record 447 yards and two touchdowns. Doug Flutie outdid that, throwing for 472 yards and three touchdowns. He also became the first quarterback to ever throw for 10,000 or more yards in a college career. But the final play will always be what Flutie is remembered for.

If the 55 Flood Tip was run like it was supposed to be, all of Flutie's receivers would run straight routes to the end zone. Then as the ball was flying to them, one of the wide receivers would tip the ball to their closest teammate for a touchdown. But as he always did for his entire college career, Doug Flutie improvised.

Flutie bounced away from a Miami defender, rolled to his right, and uncorked a pass that spiraled through the heavens. A football prayer was sailing through the air and falling back to earth… And as luck would have it, it fell right into the arms of Flutie's roommate, friend and Eagles wide receiver Gerard Phelan for the game-winning touchdown!

The play not only was an instant classic. It also locked up the Heisman Trophy for Flutie. He became the first quarterback since 1971 to win the award. But even with an incredible college career in the books, people still doubted him. They just couldn't shake the fact that he was only 5'9".
NFL executives doubted Flutie so much that he didn't even start his professional career in the NFL. He was actually selected by a team called the New Jersey Generals of the United States Football League (USFL) in January 1985.

But after the USFL folded in 1986 and Flutie bounced around in the NFL with the Bears and Patriots from 1987 to 1989, he took his talents north of the border and signed on to play in the Canadian Football League. This is where his star would shine the brightest.

In eight seasons in the CFL, Flutie would win six CFL Most Outstanding Player Awards, and three Grey Cups, the CFL equivalent to the Super Bowl in the United States. He also passed for over 41,000 yards and 271 touchdowns. After this, Flutie finally got his long-awaited chance to try to succeed in the NFL.

Flutie would make his first NFL start when he led the Buffalo Bills against the undefeated Jacksonville Jaguars on October 18, 1998. And not only did he start that game, he scored the game-winning touchdown by running the football into the end zone for the Bills!

This kicked off a run for Buffalo that included going 8-3 in games with Flutie starting at quarterback. He led them to the Playoffs, where they fell to Miami in the first round. But at 35 years old, he proved that he still had the skills that had made him a household name at Boston College, and a CFL legend and Hall of Famer north of the border in Canada.

The next year, Flutie was still red-hot. He won 10 games as a starter, and threw for over 3,100 yards and 19 touchdowns. Unexplainably though, Bills head coach Wade Phillips decided to bench Flutie in favor of his backup Rob Johnson as the team made the Playoffs. Sadly, this would mean the end of Flutie's time in Buffalo. But he continued fighting to show he belonged in the league and he would soon get his chance to get a little revenge on Buffalo for disrespecting him and letting him go. In the middle of the 2001 season, Doug Flutie was the Chargers' starting quarterback when San Diego faced Buffalo and his replacement, Rob Johnson. By this point in his career, Flutie might be considered what some people would call "over the hill." He was 39 years old. He wasn't a spring chicken anymore.

But he still had one last bit of Flutie magic up his sleeve. On the final drive of the game, Flutie was in danger of being sacked. The defender already had hold of him and was ready to take him down. Instead, he shook off the sack, escaped, and sprinted 13 yards for the game-winning touchdown!

He'd spend three more mostly uneventful seasons with the Chargers, but Doug Flutie broke the record for being the oldest player in the NFL to score two rushing touchdowns in a game at 41 years old, and the oldest player to ever score a touchdown at 42 years old!

After one final season in the league with the Patriots, Doug Flutie finally retired. For over 20 years, from his days at Boston College, to his run through the Canadian Football League, and both of his stints in the NFL, he believed in himself. He knew he was physically small, everyone had told him that countless times over his life, but he never let it get to him.

Doug Flutie made countless dazzling highlight-reel plays, wowed the crowd and was loved by his teammates and the fans for his effort. This led to legendary coach and broadcaster John Madden saying, "Inch for inch, Flutie in his prime was the best QB of his generation."

If people pick on you for any shortcoming, use it as fuel and keep grinding. Don't get mad at them. But use it to power your way to success. Keep your head down and work hard. Then when you do make it to where you want to be, just smile at them and wave. That's what Doug Flutie did. The so-called little guy played bigger than just about anybody. He's a winner at football and life. And with the same mindset as him, you can win at life too!

- Wore #22 in college because of his favorite baseball player and sports idol, pitcher Jim Palmer.

- His final play as a pro football player was a successful dropkick for a Patriots extra point.

- In 2007, Doug Flutie was inducted into Canada's Sports Hall of Fame, the first non-Canadian to ever be inducted.

- Played college football at Boston College.

- Won the 1984 Heisman Trophy.

- Even though he struggled to catch on in the NFL at times, Flutie was a legend in the Canadian Football League!

- Holds the record for most career passing yards in the Canadian Football League.

- Kicked the first successful drop kick in the NFL in decades!

- Was extremely short for a quarterback in any professional league, at just 5'9.

- His last pass in the NFL was a touchdown.

1. Where did Doug Flutie play college football?

2. What was the name of Doug Flutie's Hail Mary pass talked about in the story?

3. The NFL has the Super Bowl as its championship game. What's the name of the Canadian Football League's championship game?

4. How many Grey Cups has Doug Flutie won?

5. True or False: Doug Flutie has won six CFL MVP awards.

6. True or False: Doug Flutie played in an NFL game at 43 years old.

7. What's the name of the football video game that's named after Doug Flutie?

8. True or False: Doug Flutie has a street named after him in Massachusetts.

9. True or false: Doug Flutie is in the Pro Football Hall of Fame.

10. True or false: Doug Flutie is in the College Football Hall of Fame.

ANSWER

1. Doug Flutie played college football at Boston College for the Golden Eagles from 1981 to 1984.
2. "Hail Flutie."
3. The Grey Cup.
4. He won three Grey Cups!
5. True! Although it's not called an MVP. It's called the Most Outstanding Player Award.
6. True! At the time, he was 43, while the opposing quarterback, Vinny Testaverde, was 42 years old.
7. Doug Flutie's Maximum Football.
8. True! It's called Flutie Pass, after his 1984 Hail Mary pass against the University of Miami.
9. False.
10. True!

"It's my whole life of being the little guy and having a little chip on my shoulder, from year to year trying to prove myself, and at the end of the day to be inducted into the College Football Hall of Fame is a very special honor for me."

"The Flutie Bowl is a great event that brings together people who really care about the autism community. We always have a great time bowling and playing music."

"It's nice to have a situation where you can make it fun."

"I think the only time I doubted myself was my senior year in high school. I was not offered a Division I scholarship. I remember a scout from Ohio State coming in and looking at my film. He was all excited to meet me. Then he met me and I was 5'10" and he said that I was not a Division I quarterback."

"Any game is important to me. At Boston College, when I went out for the spring games, I wanted to win. Maybe it is more important than other preseason games. It's just that everyone is expecting a lot from me in my first week of professional football. I want to confirm my expectations."

LESSONS FROM THE STORY

- You're never too old to pursue a passion. It's never too late.

- Heart beats talent when it's combined with hard work.

- Nothing worth having ever came easy.

- There will always be obstacles in the way. How you react to them will say a lot about who you are as a person.

- It's great to have big dreams. But make sure you set and hit small daily goals too, so you can eventually achieve those big dreams!

4

VINCE PAPALE

MR. INVINCIBLE

Many fans wish they could play professional football for their favorite team. But for Vince Papale, a diehard Philadelphia Eagles fan, this impossible dream actually became a reality. On the surface, he was a just special teams player for the Eagles from 1976 to 1978. But his impact on turning around a struggling team would one day be felt by Eagles fans for generations to come.

His road to success was even harder than most. Unlike Tom Brady, Papale wasn't a star college football player. In fact, he had no college football experience, and had only played with a semi-pro team, the Philadelphia Bell, for two seasons in 1974 and 1975.

He was 30 years old by the time he made the Eagles roster as a rookie in 1976. Thirty might not seem old to you since you're still in school; but in most major sports, including in the NFL, a player who's 30 or older is considered middle-aged. The career of a football player, even a great one, is shorter than you think.

But Eagles coach Dick Vermeil was impressed enough with Papale from his time with the Philadelphia Bell that he offered Papale a roster spot. And Papale took full advantage of it. He played as a gunner, or headhunter with the Eagles, which meant it was his job to sprint downfield and quickly tackle the return man on kickoffs and punts.

This is where Papale's personality soon began to come out. In order to do his job well, he practiced and played extremely hard. Much harder than regular NFL players who already had a roster spot locked up. But his motivation for being on the team was simple: he just wanted to belong.

In an interview with ESPN years after his playing days, Papale was direct and straight to the point. "All I wanted to do was to be accepted. All I wanted to do was be part of a team. And all I ever wanted to do was be a Philadelphia Eagle. That was my dream."

Have you ever had a dream? Have you ever wanted something so bad that you'd do just about anything to achieve it? You'd face any obstacles in your way, and grab that dream, no matter what it took. That was how Vince Papale approached his time with the Philadelphia Eagles.

Approach your life the same way, with enthusiasm. Life is full of goals and dreams. Set reachable goals for yourself, like getting consistently good grades in school or eating right and being healthy. Those are smaller goals, but they add up to bigger opportunities if you achieve them.

If you get consistently good grades in school, not only will you gain the respect of your teachers, your parents will be proud of you, and you will be proud of yourself. And if you are in shape and healthy, you'll live longer to pursue even bigger dreams in your life. But it all starts with daily goals.

Before Vince became a member of the Eagles, he had a daily goal too. His daily goal was to simply make it through each practice during the team's summer two-a-day workouts. He was in the middle of the blistering heat, and was absolutely exhausted. It would have been so easy for him to throw up his hands and say "I quit." He was also competing with athletes who were bigger, stronger, and faster than he was. But none of them had a heart as big as him. They wouldn't outwork him either.

He was fighting against the odds, the hot summer weather, and some people telling him he had no business being where he was. But he never gave up. Vince made it through six rounds of preseason cuts, and achieved his lifelong dream of becoming a Philadelphia Eagle, even though he had to go through a lot of pain and doubt to get there.

And once Vince had achieved his dream, he didn't rest or sit back, and prop his feet up. He suited up, buckled his chinstrap tight and got after it! His enthusiasm carried over into the way he played football. He was full-go, all the time. He was a speedster, and when he got the chance, he wasn't afraid to lay the smackdown on somebody with a big hit!

His teammate Ron Jaworski, who was the Eagles' starting quarterback from 1977 to 1986, described Papale's playing style: "He was absolutely crazy. He was going to throw his body around. He was going to have a tough time getting out of bed on Monday. But he knew that was his role to make the team."

Vince Papale may have only played for three seasons in the NFL. He may have only registered 20 tackles, 2 fumble recoveries, and one catch for 15 yards in his entire career. But impact on both the Eagles and the NFL can be a lesson to everyone: You can make something happen in your life if you work hard enough for it.

The Eagles needed that spark from him during the mid to late 1970s. They were one of the league's worst teams. They needed more than just an experienced head coach or a new gameplan for how to win on Sundays. The team needed someone who wasn't afraid to dig deep, work hard, and show that heart mattered just as much as talent. Philly didn't need flashy players. The city and team needed someone to take them back to their roots. Vince Papale was that man. An aging special teamer lit the fire that the Eagles and their fans were desperate for.

That's why he is still so loved in Philadelphia decades later. He's now approaching 80 years old, and he still runs into people on the street who tell him they're inspired by how hard he worked to make the team. Philly is a tough, blue-collar city that embraces underdogs and hardworking people who earn what they have. Vince Papale is one of those people.

We may love our favorite superstar football players, like Patrick Mahomes, Justin Jefferson, Ja'Marr Chase, and many others. And it's definitely fun to see them make highlight-reel plays, light up the scoreboard, and make ESPN's Top 10. But it's hard for anyone to relate to them. Most people aren't born with freakish athletic talent like them. But everyone is born with their own unique talents. We're all born with certain strengths and, deep down, everyone is also born with a desire to chase whatever their dreams are. For Vince Papale, his lifelong dream was to simply make it onto the roster of his favorite football team.

He knew he wasn't going to be a superstar player. He accepted that he wasn't going to be on the team very long, if he made it at all. But just the thought of being a Philadelphia Eagle lit a fire within him that nobody could extinguish. And he used that fire to push himself until he reached his goal, and made his dream a reality.

You're young and have your entire life ahead of you to chase your dreams. What lights your fire? What are you passionate about? Whatever that passion is, chase it like Vince Papale chased his passion. Do whatever it takes to get there. Don't let self-doubt creep in. And don't listen to any of the people who tell you that you should focus on something else. If there's a dream and passion that you need to pursue in life, go for it!

BONUS

Unlock an exclusive treasure trove of football knowledge with our bonus content: 100 Unique Football Facts and Trivia Questions. This special collection will enrich your understanding of the game and provide you with captivating trivia to impress friends and family. From iconic moments in football history to intriguing facts about legendary players, this content is perfect for deepening your appreciation of the sport. Enhance your journey with these fascinating insights and become a true football aficionado. Whether you're a lifelong fan or new to the game, this bonus content will provide hours of enjoyment. Get ready to explore the wonders of football like never before.

To access your bonus content, simply scan the QR code below with your smartphone and dive into the world of football!

- Was a talented pole vaulter while attending St. Joseph's University in the 1960s.

- He's a motivational speaker.

- Worked as a TV and radio broadcaster for eight years after he retired from the NFL.

- Earned the nickname "Rocky" while he was with the team, a nod to Sylvester Stallone's famous movie character, Rocky Balboa, who is also supposed to be from Philadelphia.

- His struggle to make the team was made into a Disney movie in 2006 called *Invincible*, where he was played by Mark Wahlberg.

- Papale's story was a factor in the Eagles' decision to sign tight end Jeff Thomason to the team before they played the Patriots in Super Bowl 39. Thomason was with the Eagles from 2000 to 2002 before being cut, and he worked in construction before and after he was signed to play in the Super Bowl.

- Papale currently lives with his wife Janet, and their two children, Gabriela and Vinny, in New Jersey.

- He is currently the Secretary/Treasurer for the Philadelphia chapter of the NFL Alumni Association.

- His wife is a world-class former gymnast.

- Vince took part in the Olympic Trials in the decathlon.

1. True or false: Vince played college football before being signed by the Eagles.

2. What positions did Vince play when he was with the Eagles?

3. How many years did Vince play professional football?

4. What was the other team Vince played pro football with besides the Eagles?

5. True or false: Vince lied about his age to get a tryout with the Philadelphia Bell of the WFL.

6. Who played Vince in the 2006 movie Invincible?

7. How many tackles did Vince make during his NFL career?

8. True or false: Vince was honored and recognized by the Eagles for his career.

9. True or false: Vince was born and raised in Philadelphia.

10. Papale earned a nickname among his Eagles teammates for his stubborn work ethic and never giving up. What did they call him?

ANSWER

1. False. Vince Papale never played college football.
2. He played as a wide receiver and special teamer.
3. He played five seasons of professional football, three with the Eagles.
4. He played football with the Philadelphia Bell of the World Football League in 1974 and 1975.
5. True! Vince told the team he was 24 years old at the time instead of 28. He wanted on the team that badly!
6. Mark Wahlberg.
7. 20 tackles.
8. True! He is a member of the Philadelphia Eagles 75th Anniversary Team.
9. False.
10. Rocky. The nickname refers to Rocky Balboa, a fictional boxer who is also from Philadelphia.

"All I wanted to do was to be accepted. All I wanted to do was be part of a team. And all I ever wanted to do was to be a Philadelphia Eagle."

"It was 7-on-7, it was seven guys. Everybody was eligible to go out and make the play. And I was a speedster."

"I'm the king of 7-on-7. They can't touch me on 7-on-7. So now these guys are trying to take my head. You guys can't hurt me."

"As the season started to get closer, everybody was pulling for him. I was saying, 'Vince, you've gotta do this. You've got to get to the next day. You can't take any crap from anybody. You've gotta get up and get in their faces." -Dennis Franks, Papale's Eagles teammate.

"Other than my children and my beautiful wife, it's the greatest moment in my life." -Papale about making the team.

LESSONS FROM THE STORY

- You're never too old to pursue a passion. It's never too late.

- Heart beats talent when it's combined with hard work.

- Nothing worth having ever came easy.

- There will always be obstacles in the way. How you react to them will say a lot about who you are as a person.

- It's great to have big dreams. But make sure you set and hit small daily goals too, so you can eventually achieve those big dreams!

5

DETROIT LIONS

RESTORING THE ROAR!

It's no secret that the Detroit Lions were bad for decades. Ever since Barry Sanders disappeared from the game after the 1998 season, Lions haven't had much to cheer for since then. They would make a run to get to the playoffs here and there. But they never could put everything together. Rock bottom was in 2008, when the team finished 0-16, and posted the first winless season in NFL history.

But finally, after years and years of bad football, and snatching defeat from the jaws of victory, it looks like the Lions are finally finding their way. Head coach Dan Campbell, who played for Detroit from 2006 to 2008 as a tight end, has brought a toughness to the team that wasn't there before. Some people laughed when he was hired by the Lions in January 2021, especially when it came to his introduction.

He gave a fiery speech that talked about how the city of Detroit was full of hardworking people. He also said that just like the city, the Lions would get up from being battered, bruised, and kicked around. People laughed at his speech, and dismissed him. After all, who did this guy think he was? Detroit has stunk for years. There's no way he could put them back on the map. He'll be just another failed head coach in a long list. He won't last the season.

It looked like his critics were right; at least at first. The Lions finished the first season under him with an awful 3-13-1 record, and even went into 2022 losing six of their first seven games. But Lions owner Sheila Ford Hamp and General Manager Brad Holmes were patient. They trusted the process, they didn't make any knee-jerk reactions that would set the team back, and they had a quiet confidence in what they were doing.

And just like an old Detroit-made muscle car struggling to start, and then roaring to life, the Lions eventually caught fire, and won eight of their final 10 games. They finished 2022 at 9-8, their first winning season in five years!

Behind star players like quarterback Jared Goff, wideout Amon-Ra St. Brown, running back Jamaal Williams, and rookie pass rusher and hometown kid Aidan Hutchinson, the Lions developed a unique identity as a team—they were explosive on offense, and terrifying on defense.

And the next season, they were even better. Something happened in 2023 that hadn't happened in 30 years—the Lions won the NFC North! They had been so bad for so long that the last time they won their division as one of the NFL's best teams, was in 1993 when they won the old NFC Central.

Led by gunslinger Jared Goff, who threw for over 4,500 yards and 30 touchdowns, and a top 3 offensive unit averaging over 27 points a game, and nearly 400 yards a game, Detroit rolled to the postseason for the first time since 2016.

But if you thought the magical run for the Lions would end there, you'd be wrong. The 12-5 Lions not only won their division for the first time in three decades, but they also earned the right to host their first-ever playoff game at Ford Field, against the Los Angeles Rams. The atmosphere was already electric, but leading the Rams against Detroit was none other than Matthew Stafford, the former #1 overall pick who was drafted by the Lions, and who had spent 12 seasons trying to get the team to where they currently are. And now he'd try to break the hearts of his former fans, and lead the Rams on another deep playoff run.

But Detroit would set off some fireworks early, as they jumped out to a 14-3 lead in the first quarter. Jared Goff came out hot, and played like a Pro Bowl quarterback. He led the Lions down the field in a hurry on two consecutive touchdown drives. However, the Rams would show why they'd won the Super Bowl two years earlier with how they responded. Rookie wide receiver Puka Nacua hauled in a touchdown to cut the Detroit lead to 14-10. He would go on to have a huge night, as he hauled in nine catches for an incredible 181 yards.

When the game mattered the most, Detroit's defense stiffened up, especially in the red zone when the Rams threatened to score. They held Los Angeles to only 3 for 9 on third down, and forced a powerful Rams offense to routinely settle for field goals instead of touchdowns. They represented the city of Detroit on the football field with how they played that day—tough, gritty, relentless, and unwilling to give up. The Lions weren't the laughingstock of the NFL anymore. They were here to win.

The game eventually tightened up, and as time went on, Detroit was holding on for dear life to a one-point lead. They were up 24-23, with eight minutes left. But just like the Lions defense, the offensive unit would not be denied. Many of these players had been here through the sad 3-13-1 season when Dan Campbell took over. They knew what bad football was like and felt like. But losing a playoff game after leading it the whole way would feel worse. And they refused to blow it!

After the defense got another critical stop, Jared Goff and the offense trotted out onto the field one final time. At this point in the game, the fans at Ford Field were in an absolute frenzy! They sensed what was coming. A generational win. Older Lions fans had only seen the playoff wins in 1991 and 1957. For the rest? Many of them weren't even alive the last time Barry Sanders and his teammates gave Detroit a taste of postseason success. But the Lions needed two more first downs; otherwise, Matthew Stafford and the Rams would drive down the field and kick a game-winning field goal. But the Lions had come too far. They were too close to history to turn back now. And they did just that. The offense sealed the game. The Rams never got the ball back. Detroit held on for their biggest win in decades. They had done it.

The scene at Ford Field was like something out of a classic sports movie—fans were biting their nails right up until the final play. Then after the clock hit triple zeroes, many of them burst into tears! Grown men and women were crying. An 89-year-old man named Benjamin Capp, who had been a Lions season ticket holder since 1957 when they won their last NFL Championship, simply smiled and took in the scene that was before him.

In an absolutely ecstatic locker room, Coach Dan Campbell and GM Brad Holmes were emotional. Campbell tossed Holmes a game ball and said: "I absolutely love every single person in this room, man. We were intentional on being about grit, and earning it. I love everybody in here. We went through darkness and it shaped us. It shaped us for this moment. I love you all."

Head coach Dan Campbell also talked about building toward their current success: "When you came in three years ago, and you had a vision, you start working together. You get an idea how you want to build it, and you go from top to bottom. It's a crappy business sometimes. It ain't always perfect. But we do a pretty good job."

The Lions' early struggles shaped the success they're having right now. And your struggles in life, whatever they may be, can shape your future success. It does not matter how much you are struggling. It does not matter how far away you feel from achieving your goals. Persistence, patience, and a relentless work ethic can always get you to where you want to be. Take a cue from the Detroit Lions: With the right people surrounding you in life, success of any kind is never out of reach.

No matter where you are in life, you can achieve your dreams. Continue to work at them, even if you are struggling now. One day, your time will come. Don't listen to the doubters. Don't listen to the people who are laughing at you. They don't know what your dream is. They aren't on the same journey as you are. They haven't had to struggle, fail, fall on their face, and get back up like you have. They don't know what you're going through on the road to success.

But you do. You know what it takes. The people supporting you also know you and your dreams, and if they are truly in your corner and on your team, they will help push you to the top of the mountain. But it all starts with your belief in yourself. So, get up, dust yourself off, and move forward with the heart of a Lion!

- Started 8-2 for the first time since 1962.

- Won a Playoff game for the first time since 1992.

- Got as close as they've ever been to the Super Bowl. Unfortunately lost to the San Francisco 49ers in the NFC Championship Game, 34-31.

- The Lions won the NFC North Championship for the first time in their history.

- They went 12-5, which is one of the best records in team history.

- They appeared in the NFC Championship Game for the first time since the 1991 season.

- Had seven Pro Bowlers on the team in 2023.

- Defeated their former quarterback Matthew Stafford in the Playoffs. He played for the Rams, who the Lions beat in the Wild Card round.

- Lions tight end Sam LaPorta had one of the best seasons for a rookie tight end in NFL history!

- 2023 was the team's second straight winning season under coach Dan Campbell

1. Who did the Lions lose to in the NFC Championship Game?

2. True or false: Jahmyr Gibbs, Detroit's rookie running back, made the Pro Bowl in his first season.

3. Who owns the Lions?

4. True or False: Sheila Ford Hamp, is descended from Henry Ford.

5. True or false: Head coach Dan Campbell has now been both a player and head coach for the Detroit Lions.

6. True or False: Dan Campbell was named the NFL Head Coach of the Year in 2023.

7. Dan Campbell had a famous nickname during his playing career. What was it?

8. True or False: The Lions were ranked in the Top 5 in offense in 2023.

9. True or False: The Lions defeated the Kansas City Chiefs to open the year.

10. True or false: Lions quarterback Jared Goff did so well in 2023, he made the Pro Bowl!

ANSWER

1. The San Francisco 49ers.
2. True!
3. Sheila Ford Hamp.
4. True!
5. True! He was with the team as a player from 2006-2008.
6. False. Cleveland's Kevin Stefanski won that honor, but Dan Campbell is one of the best new coaches in the game today!
7. The Dude. He looked like Jeff Bridges' character from The Big Lebowski.
8. True!
9. True!
10. False.

"We're going to do something special, gentlemen, and we will never forget this season. Ever."

"This team is going to take on the identity of this city. This city's been down, but it's found a way to get up."

"To take the next step, you're shooting for the Division. I think we're positioned to swing with the big boys this year."

"When we play well, we can compete with anybody."

"I absolutely love every single person in this room, man. We were intentional on being about grit, and earning it. I love everybody in here. We went through darkness and it shaped us. It shaped us for this moment. I love you all."

LESSONS FROM THE STORY

- Even if you are struggling to reach your goals and dreams now, don't give up!

- People who don't know your journey are going to talk behind your back. Don't listen to them.

- Build a support system of family and friends who will support you on your journey.

- Some days you will feel down and discouraged. Keep going!

- The people who are with you and supporting you when you've just started your journey, deserve to be with you when you reach the top. Never forget them!

6

THE CLEVELAND SUMMIT

BRAVERY IN ACTION

Today, many athletes are superstars. They're loved by so many people around the world and respected for their views on many things. Thanks to the First Amendment in America, everyone is free to have any opinion they want without being afraid of getting in serious trouble for it. But that wasn't the case for Jim Brown retired from football in 1966, and went into acting in 1967.

You see, not only was Jim Brown arguably the greatest running back of all time, but he was also a civil rights icon in his prime, too. It's easier for today's athletes to preach about social activism when a large chunk of society supports them. But it took far more courage and conviction for Jim to stand up for an unpopular stance in America in the mid-to-late 1960s, especially as a Black man.

It didn't matter if he was a football megastar. Racism and injustice were still very, very real at that time in the United States, even against famous Black athletes such as himself. And one of these injustices happened when the United States Government punished Muhammad Ali for his refusal to be inducted into the Army to fight in the Vietnam War. Ali was arrested, his boxing license was revoked, and he was stripped of his title as the Heavyweight Champion of the World.

Jim Brown then decided to host what became known as the Cleveland Summit in the backroom of his business, the Black Economic Union, in Cleveland, Ohio. On June 4, 1967, Brown and other famous Black athletes and political figures gathered there to decide whether to publicly support Muhammad Ali in his fight against the government.

In an interview years later, Brown discussed the reason for the Cleveland Summit, as well as what everyone there stood to lose in terms of popularity and getting into legal trouble. Everyone at the Summit had something on the line that they stood to lose if Muhammad Ali lost his fight with the government. But they decided to support him anyway. "We thought that he had the right as an American citizen to be a conscientious objector, and to use his religion in that way. But the United States Government was going to prosecute him with everything they had."

Jim Brown decided that he was willing to put his fame and popularity on the line to support his friend, and he was ready to urge other Black sports superstars to do the same. "I felt that if I could get some of the top Black athletes in the country to come together, and have a public meeting with him to get his full views. If we believed him and trusted him, we could back him up at the risk of whatever we had to take."

With his mind made up, Jim Brown invited several other prominent sports superstars of the day to join him and Ali at the Summit in Cleveland, they included:

Kareem Abdul-Jabbar. Six-time NBA Champion, 19-time All-Star and Hall of Famer.

Walter Beach. Former NFL player from 1960 to 1966, and one of Jim Brown's former Cleveland teammates.

Willie Davis. NFL player from 1958 to 1969, two-time Super Bowl Champion with the Green Bay Packers, Hall of Famer and one of Jim Brown's former Cleveland teammates.

Curtis McClinton. NFL player from 1962 to 1969 for the Kansas City Chiefs.

Bobby Mitchell. NFL player from 1958 to 1968, four-time Pro Bowler, Hall of Famer, and one of Jim Brown's former Cleveland teammates.

Bill Russell. 11-time NBA Champion and 12-time All-Star with the Boston Celtics from 1956 to 1969. Hall of Famer.

Jim Shorter. NFL player from 1962 to 1969 with the Browns, Redskins and Steelers. One of Jim Brown's former Cleveland teammates.

Carl Stokes. A mayoral candidate for Cleveland at the time. He ended up being elected Mayor of Cleveland on November 7, 1967. He was one of the first Black mayors of any major US city.

Sidney Williams. NFL player from 1964 to 1969. Two-time NFL Champion with the Browns and Colts. One of Jim Brown's former Cleveland teammates.

John Wooten. NFL player from 1959 to 1968. NFL Champion with the Browns in 1964, and two-time Super Bowl Champion with the Cowboys and Ravens as a member of their front office staff. One of Jim Brown's former Cleveland teammates.

Many of the men attending the Summit initially were very skeptical and unsure about supporting Ali in his fight against the government. Most of them were also military veterans, and criticizing the Vietnam War in 1967 was seen as "unpatriotic" by many Americans. But over the course of the hours-long meeting, Ali defended his position by answering several questions from the others who were there, including Jim Brown. By the end of it, Ali had convinced them to come out in support of his decision to refuse induction into the Army.

If you still don't understand just how big the Cleveland Summit was in Civil Rights and sports history, let me show you just what Jim Brown and the other men were risking by siding with Ali. Let me give you an example from today that might be comparable.

The NBA has a huge presence in China. But the Chinese government has also been accused of violating human rights. If LeBron James and other megastars in the world of sports spoke out against China, they'd risk not only losing money, but they would also risk losing millions of fans. Jim Brown and the others at the Cleveland Summit risked not only those things, but they also risked possible legal action as well. But they stood in solidarity with their friend and fellow athlete.

In the end, the show of support that Jim Brown and the other athletes gave to Muhammad Ali eventually caused the government to drop their case against him. His boxing license was reinstated, and he was free to exercise his religious beliefs, even if it meant protesting the Vietnam War as an unjust war.

But who knows what would have happened if Muhammad Ali was forced to fight this battle on his own? He was a brave man and fierce in his convictions and beliefs. But without the Cleveland Summit, and every man at the meeting, he may not have been successful in getting the government off his back. It took courage for Ali to stand up for what he believed in, and he should always be remembered and praised for his courage. The man overcame every tough situation that he found himself in. But Jim Brown should also be honored and remembered for organizing the Cleveland Summit, one of the most famous gatherings of Black athletes in American history. As should every other man who was brave enough to participate in the Summit.

The message of the story here is simple: If you see something that is wrong in your world, have the courage to speak up and act. Yes, it may be hard. Yes, there may be sacrifices you have to make. But true courage is rare in today's world. It's easy to go along with the crowd and protest when hundreds or even thousands of people are protesting something.

But what if society is against something you know is right? Would you have the courage to stand up for it, even if you were completely alone or only supported by your closest friends and family? To stand up in the face of genuine injustice all by yourself takes real courage. It takes guts to do the right thing, especially when not many people are doing it, or you have a view that not many people agree with.

But Jim Brown, Muhammad Ali, and every man at the Cleveland Summit are heroes to many because they saw an injustice in their world, and tackled it head on. They didn't hesitate because of their bank accounts, personal safety, or reputations as superstars; they simply used their influence to do the right thing.

If you do the right thing, and show courage in the face of injustice, who knows how many people you can inspire? The world needs more heroes. Be brave, and be one of them today!

FUN FACTS ABOUT THE CLEVELAND SUMMIT

- The Cleveland Summit was a closed-door meeting of the greatest Black athletes and celebrities of the time.

- The meeting was held on June 4, 1967, by superstar Cleveland Browns running back Jim Brown.

- The meeting was held to decide if the other Black athletes and celebrities would support Muhammad Ali in his refusal to fight in the Vietnam War

- Boxing promoter Bob Arum worked out a deal with the US Government to drop Ali's draft evasion charges. If Ali fought in exhibition bouts for the troops, his charges would be dropped.

- The Nation of Islam, a fringe religious movement reportedly would have paid off some of the athletes who were at the Summit, if they convinced Ali to accept being drafted into the Army. Ali obviously did not take the deal.

- In September 2023, the Summit was officially included as part of the Cleveland Civil Rights Trail, when a plaque was introduced near Cleveland Browns Stadium. The plaque describes the Summit as "one of the most important civil rights acts in sports history."

- Many of the attendees were former Browns teammates of Jim Brown, who played for Cleveland from 1957 to 1965.

- This was one of the most high-profile events of the Civil Rights Movement of the 1960s.

- Every person there was risking their reputation and professional career by supporting Muhammad Ali.

- Ali's protest of the war, and refusal to be drafted to fight in Vietnam, was seen as unpopular by many people. He was seen as unpatriotic.

1. What was the name of the building where the Cleveland Summit took place?

2. True or false: The people at the meeting were extremely supportive of Ali right off the bat.

3. True or False: Famous NBA player Kareem Abdul-Jabbar was one of the men at the meeting.

4. True or false: Many of the men at the meeting were ex-military members.

5. True or false: A deal was in place for Ali to perform exhibition boxing matches for troops, in exchange for his charges being dropped.

6. True or false: Ali eventually compromised at the meeting and backed down.

7. True or false: The jury that found Ali guilty of draft evasion was composed entirely of White people.

8. True or false: Ali was later exiled from boxing for three more years.

9. When were the charges against Ali dropped?

10. True or false: Ali later won the Heavyweight Championship of the World one more time in his career.

ANSWER

1. *The Black Economic Union.*
2. *False. Many were skeptical.*
3. *True! Although he went by Lew Alcindor at the time.*
4. *True!*
5. *True.*
6. *False.*
7. *True.*
8. *True.*
9. *1971.*
10. *True!*

"He has something I have never been able to attain and something very few people I know possess," Russell wrote. "He has an absolute and sincere faith. ... I'm not worried about Muhammad Ali. He is better equipped than anyone I know to withstand the trials in store for him. What I'm worried about is the rest of us." -Bill Russell.

"The Champ is sincere in his religious beliefs. He believes sincerely in his religion, and his stand is based wholly on that." -Jim Brown.

"During those hours, he said he was sincere, and his religion was important to him. He convinced all of us, even someone like me, who was suspicious. We weren't easy on him. We wanted Ali to understand what he was getting himself into. He convinced us that he was." -Bobby Mitchell

"They said, 'We're going to support him. We're going to support his right to be a conscientious objector.' And they had that press conference afterward and showing that support." -Branson Wright.

"The Cleveland Summit was the first — and last — time that so many African American athletes at that level came together to support a controversial cause." -William C. Rhoden

LESSONS FROM THE STORY

- Many of today's celebrities aren't as brave as they used to be.

- It's easy to go along with the crowd. It's harder to speak up for what you believe in.

- If you see something wrong, don't be afraid to speak up!

- Support your friends when they need you the most.

- Sacrifices must sometimes be made in order to do the right thing.

7

GALE SAYERS AND BRIAN PICCOLO

AN UNLIKELY FRIENDSHIP

If we have a few real friends in life, we are blessed, and Chicago Bears teammates Gale Sayers and Brian Piccolo were the definition of true friends. Piccolo and Sayers became friends in the mid-1960s, and were very close during their time in Chicago. Their friendship continued, even though they both went through some of the lowest points in Chicago Bears history on some bad teams. But their friendship also was a very rare example of a Black man and White man getting along, considering the time.

Race relations during the 1960s and 1970s wasn't just tense; race relations were probably at their worst since the Civil War. However, Gale Sayers and Brian Piccolo were different. At first, they didn't like each other; they were polar opposites. Brian was an outgoing, talkative prankster, and Gale was a quiet man who didn't say much. Sayers was so quiet that Piccolo once thought of him as arrogant.

If you also look at where they came from before they arrived in Chicago, their careers were opposites as well. Gale Sayers was a first-round pick nicknamed the "Kansas Comet" when he played college football for the Jayhawks, while Brian Piccolo was an undrafted free agent just struggling to find his place in the NFL. But once they became roommates in 1967, they helped break barriers not only for the Chicago Bears, but for the rest of the NFL as well during a very tense, uneasy time. For other NFL teams at the time, the players were still segregated by skin color.

When Bears coach George Halas was trying to rebuild a struggling team, he decided that players in the same position group should room together. Quarterbacks would room with other quarterbacks, wide receivers would room with other wide receivers, and so on. As fate would have it, Sayers and Piccolo were the first Black and White running back duo to be roommates in NFL history. However, the two men would show that their friendship was about more than just skin color. Particularly when Sayers suffered a serious knee injury in a game against the San Francisco 49ers in November 1968.

Most people in Brian Piccolo's position would probably be hungry to steal the spotlight and the job from an injured teammate. Could anybody blame them? After all, the NFL is extremely competitive. Unless you are freakishly athletic, huge and fast, it's really tough to make an NFL roster. But surprisingly, Brian didn't steal Gale Sayers' job as Chicago's starting running back. Instead, he personally helped him rehab his injured knee. Brian would play as the main running back when Gale was out. One time, he even ran for 160 yards! But he was more focused on helping his teammate and friend recover fully, so that the Bears would be stronger going forward.

As if to reward Piccolo for helping Sayers get back to health, Bears coach George Halas later named Piccolo the starting fullback. This meant that they both would be on the field at the same time. Piccolo was #41, and was responsible for clearing the way for Sayers, who wore #40. Piccolo's job as a fullback was to either block for Sayers, catch passes out of the backfield, or run the ball when the Bears were close to scoring a touchdown. But the two men were often working side by side. This was extremely rare not just in the NFL, but in sports in general during the mid-to-late 1960s.

But just as Piccolo was there for Sayers when he was rehabbing his knee, Brian would soon need Gale's help for a much bigger battle. Brian Piccolo only stood six feet tall, and weighed just over 200 pounds. This was small for a fullback at the time, and is still considered undersized for a player in most positions today. But Piccolo was a competitor. He ran hard and gave everything he had. And he never took himself out of a game. That is until he did so in 1969 in Atlanta against the Falcons. This would signal that something was very wrong.

Brian not only stopped playing, but he also had trouble even breathing, which meant he was sent to the doctor once the Bears arrived back in Chicago after the game. Sadly, he received the worst news someone could possibly get: he was dying from a rare form of cancer at just 26 years old. This was Gale Sayers' chance to return the favor. He had a chance to be by his friend's side as he battled for his life against cancer. And that's exactly what he did. Gale routinely checked in on Brian as he went through three operations, chemotherapy, and other treatments. But it's what Gale did next that showed how much Brian meant to him as a friend.

After recovering from his knee injury and playing a lot better in 1969, Gale Sayers received the George S. Halas Award, which is awarded by the Bears to the player who is the most courageous. But instead of making an acceptance speech for the award, Gale instead says the award should be given to Brian. By this point, Brian is in the hospital, and very sick with cancer. But Gale talks about how brave Brian is for continuing to fight his cancer: "He has the heart of a giant. And a rare form of courage which allows him to kid himself, and his opponent, cancer. He has a mental attitude which makes me proud to have a friend who spells out courage 24 hours a day, every day for the rest of his life. Brian Piccolo is the man of courage who should receive the George S. Halas award. It's mine tonight. And Brian Piccolo's tomorrow. I love Brian Piccolo. And I'd like all of you to love him too. And tonight, when you hit your knees, please ask God to love him."

On June 16, 1970, Brian Piccolo passed away after his battle with the disease. He was only 26 years old. It would be 50 years until Gale Sayers would be reunited with his friend on that Great Football Field in the Sky. Gale passed away on September 23, 2020, at 77 years old. But the legacy and friendship that both men shared is immortalized in sports history forever. And not just because of the great sports movie *Brian's Song*, but more importantly, their friendship symbolized what can happen when two people from completely different backgrounds treat each other with kindness and respect.

They were very different men. One was White and struggling to get his career of the ground, while the other was Black, and expected to be a star player. But they formed the most unlikely friendship when it was frowned up and discouraged for Black people and White people to even talk to each other. Let alone be friends. But Gale and Brian didn't let the world tell them their friendship was wrong. In fact, they showed the world that it had a lot of learning and growing to do.

Their friendship can teach us a lot about the world we live in today, too. People find it really hard to be respectful to each other about anything. They are more focused on being right, rather than being kind to each other. People see each other's differences in 2024 America as a bad thing, or something to be made fun of.

But the friendship that Brian Piccolo and Gale Sayers had during a time that was even worse, shows us that love and kindness do exist. Even in places where we least expect to find them. You can mirror the relationship that Brian had with Gale by talking to or being friends with someone very different from you. It's easy to be friends with people who think, act, and look like you do. But you might learn more and grow more as a person if you go out of your comfort zone to be kind to others you might not normally hang out with.

Go out of your way to talk to and be kind to those people. Go out of your way to sit next to the lonely kid who has no friends during lunch. They need kindness more than you know. The world needs more kindness toward people we might not normally talk to or be friends with. When the world teaches you to judge others for dumb reasons, be a bigger person, and show the world that it needs to do better. Brian Piccolo and Gale Sayers certainly did. And they'd be proud of you if you did the same!

- Gale Sayers originally wanted to play himself in the movie Brian's Song, but his training camp schedule wouldn't allow for him to do it.

- Brian Piccolo actually led the country in rushing yards and rushing touchdowns his senior season at Wake Forest in 1964. He rushed for 1,044 yards and 17 touchdowns and was named ACC Player of the Year. Surprisingly, Piccolo went undrafted in both the AFL and NFL drafts.

- Brian Piccolo considered baseball his primary sport until about halfway through high school.

- Gale Sayers was drafted in the first round, while Brian Piccolo signed with the Bears as a free agent.

- They were the first integrated roommates in NFL history at the time.

- The George S. Halas Award was given to the Bears player who showed the greatest example of courage every season.

- Gale Sayers received the award in 1970 after recovering from a knee injury, but instead of taking the award for himself, he dedicated it to his friend, Brian Piccolo.

- Brian Piccolo passed away at the young age of 26 years old in 1970.

- Gale Sayers lived to be 77 years old before he passed away in 2020.

- Gale Sayers and Brian Piccolo were polar opposites in terms of personality, but they were great friends on and off the field.

1. Which colleges did Brian Piccolo and Gale Sayers go to?

2. What number did Gale Sayers wear?

3. What number did Brian Piccolo wear?

4. How many Pro Bowls did Gale Sayers appear in during his career?

5. What was the name of the movie based on Brian Piccolo's life?

6. True or false: Gale Sayers and Brian Piccolo instantly got along when they first met each other.

7. What was Brian Piccolo's nickname among his teammates?

8. What was Gale Sayers' nickname in college?

9. Which disease did Brian Piccolo fight bravely?

10. True or false: Brian Piccolo and Gale Sayers eventually played in the same backfield together while with the Bears.

ANSWER

1. Gale Sayers played college football at Kansas, while Brian Piccolo played college football at Wake Forest.
2. 40.
3. 41.
4. Four Pro Bowls.
5. Brian's Song.
6. False. Gale thought Brian was too talkative, while Brian thought Gale didn't like him because he didn't say much.
7. Pic.
8. The Kansas Comet.
9. Cancer
10. True! Brian wore #41 and was a blocking fullback, while Gale wore #40 and was the running back.

"Four hundred and forty draftees and none of 'em me," Piccolo said. "I was disappointed and embarrassed. Really embarrassed." -Brian Piccolo

"I don't like practice. But the competition, the game, it's glorious. You're doing something you love." -Brian Piccolo

"You have to be in the right place at the right time," In my case, I happened to be a running back and they happened to draft Gale Sayers the same year. That's not exactly the best way to bust into the league. That's not exactly what you'd call being in the right place at the right time." -Brian Piccolo

"Pic never badmouthed anybody. They say that people who like themselves like other people, and Brian was never short on self-confidence. He truly liked people." -Gale Sayers

"He has the heart of a giant and that rare form of courage that allows him to kid himself and his opponent -- cancer," Sayers told the audience. "He has the mental attitude that makes me proud to have a friend who spells out the word 'courage' 24 hours a day of his life. I love Brian Piccolo, and I'd like all of you to love him, too. Tonight, when you hit your knees, please ask God to love him." -Gale Sayers

LESSONS FROM THE STORY

• True friendship can cross all kinds of boundaries.

• Friends always have each other's back in good times and in bad times.

• You find out who is there for you when you're at rock bottom and at your worst.

• People from two completely different backgrounds can be best friends!

• Try to make friends with people who are completely different from you.

8

WALTER PAYTON

A LESSON IN SELFLESSNESS FROM SWEETNESS

Chicago Bears running back Walter Payton may not have been very big for an NFL player. He stood just 5'10" and weighed 200 pounds. But he ran with such power, strength, and speed that he punished anyone who tried to take him down. If he was a bruising football player, why was this Hall of Fame running back nicknamed "Sweetness"? Well, that depends on who you ask. Some say he earned the nickname during his college football days at Jackson State, where Sweetness was a twist on the nickname "Sugarman" while he played for the Tigers. Others have said Payton earned the nickname Sweetness thanks to something he shouted to a defender who tried and failed to tackle him: "Sweetness is your weakness!"

Now that he's no longer around, the nickname Sweetness fits Walter Payton to a tee. For a 200-pound man, he ran like he was bigger on the football field. But off it, he had an even bigger heart. Many athletes and celebrities today are selfish, and only care about themselves, their inner circle, and their bank accounts. But Walter Payton was different. He cared about others around him. Along with his family, he cared about his teammates as well. He wasn't in Chicago for 13 seasons just to collect a paycheck.

Even though the NFL is a hyper-competitive league, and is the highest level of football in the world, when Walter Payton played for the Chicago Bears from 1975 to 1987, he always wanted to make sure that his teammates were loose, calm, and able to do their best. One way he did this was by playing practical jokes and pranks on his teammates and the coaching staff. NFL coach Ron Rivera was a rookie with the Bears in 1984 when he told the story of how the Hall of Famer pranked him.

Bears rookies at that time always had to go get donuts in the morning, along with coffee, orange juice, and other things for the more experienced players. Ron Rivera knew this, and thought he had gotten everything in time. But Walter Payton was already in the locker room; he had arrived early.

"One thing you never were, you were never late," Rivera said. "I thought I was really early, but Walter was waiting. So I gave him the donuts, ran back to my car to get the hot chocolate, milk, orange juice and apple juice and come back in. So he hands me this glazed donut that looked like it had extra glaze on it. I grabbed it and took a big bite. As soon as I bit into it, I knew it. I should have known better. Walter had dipped it into hot wax. It tasted pretty bad. Being a rookie, Walter was out to get us. But you really felt like you were one of the guys, since they were willing to play a prank on you and have a good time at your expense."

Walter Payton used pranks like these to strengthen the camaraderie between him and the rest of his Bears teammates. But even though he loved to have fun, when it came time for kickoff? He was all business. It didn't matter who the Bears were playing, Payton carried on the tradition of the man who came before him, Gayle Sayers, when it came to tough Chicago running backs. Like Sayers, Payton was strong, fast, extremely powerful, and a nightmare for opposing defenders to tackle. However, Sweetness also had another weapon in his toolbox: the stutter step. Unlike a regular running back, Walter Payton used the stutter step to perfection. Whenever a defender would come at him, he would stop his stride and change direction instantly.

This often left defenders bouncing off him, missing tackles and falling on their face. If they wanted to take him down, they had to guess correctly on which direction he was going, and take the right angle to tackle him. And even if defenders did match him step for step, he punished them. It often took three or four defenders to bring him down, and he would be fighting for extra yards until he was either shoved out of bounds, or finally yanked to the ground. He was a force of nature with a competitive spirit that could not be denied or quenched.

This led to him rushing for 16,726 yards and 110 touchdowns. Both of these were records at the time of his retirement in 1987. He accomplished so many things in his storied career, including being named a nine-time Pro Bowler from 1976 to 1980, and 1983 to 1986. In the middle of that run in 1977, he also had an MVP season, where he rushed for over 1,800 yards and 14 touchdowns in just 14 games.

In 1985, Payton ran for over 1,500 yards and nine touchdowns. But most importantly, he was the key offensive player on the Bears' only Super Bowl Championship team.

Ironically, even though Walter Payton had another fantastic season that year, he only managed to run for 61 yards in Super Bowl 20 against the Patriots, and didn't score a touchdown in the game. New England slowed him down. But it didn't matter. The Bears still destroyed the Patriots 46-10.

He may have had a quiet game himself. But just the fact that Walter Payton was out there allowed his other teammates to shine. New England focused so much on stopping him that it allowed other guys to have big games instead. Wide receiver Willie Gault had the most yards that day. He caught four passes for 129 yards. Bears quarterback Jim McMahon also scored two rushing touchdowns of his own. But even though things went about as well as they possibly could for the Bears that day in New Orleans, former Chicago head coach Mike Ditka still has one big regret about that game almost 40 years later: Not letting Walter Payton score a touchdown in the Super Bowl.

"I apologized to him. I didn't think it was that important," Ditka said. "I really was worried about winning the football game, winning the Super Bowl. It never came to my mind. I made a gross mistake."

Payton's feelings were a little hurt since he didn't get a chance to score. But it didn't last long. "I was upset. A little hurt," he said. "Was. Not now. I got over it right away. You know how it is. You work all these years, you want to do well in a big game, and then, something like that takes away from the moment."

But even though Walter Payton's crowning achievement of his football career came with winning Super Bowl 20 with his teammates, the biggest impact of his life would be felt off the field. Especially when tragedy struck.

In early 1999, Walter Payton announced that he had diagnosed with cancer. But even though he was on borrowed time, he spent the last several months of his life advocating for people to become organ donors. Walter Payton's cancer was too far advanced for him to be saved, and he tragically passed away at 46 years old on November 1, 1999. But even though he had passed away, he spent his last few months alive tirelessly advocating for others instead of trying to save his own life. And even now, his foundation, the Walter and Connie Payton Foundation, keeps his legacy going by helping the less fortunate in Chicago live their best lives. The foundation also donates toys to needy kids at Christmastime to spread joy during the season.

For his big heart and caring nature, the NFL also honors him every year by choosing the winner of the Walter Payton NFL Man of the Year Award. Every NFL team nominates their representative for the award, and the winner is chosen based on the charitable impact they've made in their city, as well as their impact on the field. If a player wins the award, $250,000 is donated to the charity of their choice, while every other nominee has a $50,000 donation given to their charity. $1.8 million in total is given to charity per year.

Walter Payton was a selfless man during his lifetime. I'm sure he knew the kind of physical and athletic gifts that he had, but that didn't seem as important to him as how he impacted others. To his teammates, he was a brother and friend. To Chicago, he was one of their own. And to the rest of the NFL and the world, he was Sweetness, the man with a big playing style, but an even bigger heart!

You may or may not be athletic. That's okay. It costs nothing to be kind and selfless toward others. Only an open heart, a willingness to give, and an opportunity to do so. Sit next to the kid with no friends at lunch. Share your time with people who are struggling. Donate to your local charity. Any one of these would be great! And they would emulate Walter Payton and make him smile!

- Broke OJ Simpson's single-game NFL rushing record while he had a 101-degree fever and a bad case of the flu. He ran for 275 yards against Minnesota that day.

- Walter Payton retired in 1987, only after breaking Jim Brown's all-time leading rushing record.

- Walter Payton holds 27 different Bears records, including the lead in all-time rushing touchdowns and rushing yards.

- He was small for an NFL running back at just 5'10 and 200 pounds.

- He is a member of both the College Football and Pro Football Halls of Fame.

- Drafted by the Chicago Bears with the fourth overall pick of the 1975 NFL Draft.

- He made the Pro Bowl nine times.

- He appeared in Super Bowl 20, and won a title with the Bears.

- He was the NFL's all-time leading rusher until Emmitt Smith eventually broke his record.

- He was known for his extremely physical, punishing running style. He preferred to go through people instead of around them!

1. What was Walter Payton's nickname?

2. True or false: Walter Payton scored a touchdown in Super Bowl 20.

3. Where did Walter Payton play college football?

4. True or false: Walter Payton was a prankster, and often loved pulling jokes on his teammates and friends.

5. What is the name of Walter Payton's biography?

6. Which disease did Walter Payton pass away from?

7. Whose rushing record did Walter Payton break just before he retired from football?

8. How many career rushing yards did Walter Payton have?

9. How many career rushing touchdowns did Walter Payton have?

10. When was Walter Payton inducted into the Pro Football Hall of Fame?

ANSWER

1. Sweetness
2. False.
3. Jackson State
4. True!
5. The name of his biography is Never Die Easy.
6. Cancer.
7. Jim Brown.
8. 16,726 yards.
9. 110 rushing touchdowns.
10. 1993.

QUOTES

"When you're good at something, you'll tell everybody. When you're great at something, they'll tell you."

"If you ask me how I want to be remembered, it is as a winner. You know what a winner is? A winner is somebody who has given his best effort, who has tried the hardest they possibly can, who has utilized every ounce of energy and strength within them to accomplish something."

"Do anything that might make the world a better place for someone."

"Most important thought, if you love someone, tell him or her, for you never know what tomorrow may have in store."

"All people, regardless of whether they're athletes or not, should treat people the way they want to be treated."

LESSONS FROM THE STORY

- Give everything you have to what you're doing in this moment.

- Be selfless. Think of others before yourself.

- Be kind to everyone, or at least try as best as you can to do that.

- Learn when to take life seriously and when to have fun.

- Take compliments humbly, but then shine the spotlight on other people.

9

PAT TILLMAN

PASSION AND PATRIOTISM

Pat Tillman was a fierce competitor. Whether it was playing for the Arizona State Sun Devils in college, or for the Arizona Cardinals in the NFL, he always gave everything he had to the game of football. He was comparatively small for a linebacker, only standing 5'11" and weighing just over 200 pounds. But he was known for his wild energy, leadership, and for being an extremely hard hitter. He played the game with incredible passion.

But that was also how Pat Tillman lived his life off the football field as well. He was passionate and had a zest and enthusiasm for life that could not be toned down. In an interview recorded the day after the 9/11 attacks, Tillman explained his life and football philosophy: "Passion is kind of an important word for me. Whether it's playing sports or just living, whatever you're going to do, you should be passionate about it. Or else why do it?"

Along with living life with a ton of passion and energy, Pat Tillman was always challenging himself, and challenging others to be the best versions of themselves that they could possibly be. He was often told he was too small and slow to play football. But once he had a chance to play big-time football, the way he approached the game elevated his teammates. He was the heart of whatever defense he played on.

Linebackers are often the "quarterbacks of the defense." They make sure their teammates are in the best position to succeed, they make sure everyone knows what their role in the next play is, and they try to outsmart whatever scheme the offense is trying to run. But Pat Tillman didn't just do all those things, he also was humble and selfless as well. He made sure to give his teammates all the credit, no matter if he had a great game or not.

Pat Tillman's humility wasn't an act. He didn't care what other people thought of him, so he didn't fake acting humble to try to put on a show. Being humble was his style. Which was quite the contrast from the intimidating, violent linebacker he became when the ball was snapped! But Pat Tillman's humility and leadership would shine even more brightly after 9/11 happened. By the time the attacks happened, Pat Tillman was making a name for himself as the starting free safety for the Arizona Cardinals, and he was in line for a nice payday. All he had to do was sign his name on the dotted line of a $3.6 million contract, and he'd be set for the rest of his life.

He had always dreamed of carving out a legendary career for himself as a football player, and eventually starting a family with his high school sweetheart, Marie Tillman. All he

had to do was sign the contract. But he couldn't. He couldn't bring himself to do it. Why? His genuine love for America, and belief in what the country stood for. His home was under attack, and he chose to stand up and defend it at all costs.

"We play football, and it is so unimportant. Times like this, you stop and think about not only how good we have it, but what kind of system we live under, and what freedoms we're allowed. And that wasn't built overnight."

Tillman also felt a duty to carry on the legacy of his family by choosing to serve. "My great grandfather was at Pearl Harbor, and a lot of my family has gone and fought in wars. And I really haven't done a thing as far as laying myself on the line like that. So I have a great deal of respect for those that have, and what the flag stands for."

While many athletes in America and the world today do a lot of philanthropic work and serve others through charity, how many of them would make the sacrifice that Pat Tillman decided to make? He was just coming into his prime as a professional football player. He was 26 years old when he enlisted in 2002. He was turning down millions. And he likely would have had a solid, or even great career as a starting safety in the NFL had he kept playing. Very few athletes, if any in today's sports landscape, would do what Pat Tillman did.

And not only did he serve one tour of duty in Iraq, he chose to serve a second tour of duty, this time in Afghanistan. He turned down another opportunity to play football to go back to the frontlines and continue fighting. Even if he didn't know it at the time, this decision would ultimately cost him his life. On April 22nd, 2004, Pat Tillman and his unit, the Army's 2nd Ranger Battalion, were on patrol when he was accidentally killed by friendly fire. He was just 27 years old.

There are still questions surrounding what exactly happened when he died. But one thing that can never be questioned was Pat's love for America, and all the ideals she stands for as a country. Even though it's been 20 years since his death, Pat Tillman's devotion to duty, love of country, and passion for life and football can inspire us all to emulate those qualities in our own lives.

What are you most passionate about? Is it a sport? Is it a hobby? Is it a career you want to have when you grow up? Whatever it may be, go for it. Completely. Toss yourself into whatever you're passionate about like Pat Tillman would toss himself at an opposing receiver or running back! Give everything you have toward whatever you choose to do!

Even though he was smaller for an NFL player, Pat would always be the hardest hitter on his team. He wasn't hesitant about getting up close and personal with opposing players. In the same way, once you find something that makes you excited and like it might be your purpose, don't hesitate to go after it. Attack it with passion and enthusiasm. That would make Pat Tillman proud.

And if you do eventually follow in Pat's footsteps, and choose to serve in the military, make sure that you do it for the right reasons. Some people join up to help pay for college, and that's fine. Others might join up because they have few other prospects, or feel like they need to belong somewhere. Both of these reasons for going into the military make sense, too. But Pat Tillman joined the Army because he genuinely loved America, and all she stands for as a nation. He was an outspoken critic of the government and was never afraid to speak his mind. But was a true Patriot for loving the ideals of this country.

Lastly, be humble toward others and be a good teammate in your own life. Even if you're great at something, be gracious in both victory and defeat. Pat Tillman was a tough, hard-hitting outspoken football player. He wasn't afraid to compete as hard as he could when it came time to play. He was fiery! But either after the game, or off the field, he would often defer to his teammates when asked about his own individual performances. And he was a teammate that people loved to be around.

Jake Plummer was a former Arizona State quarterback and teammate of Pat Tillman, and knew him extremely well. The two were good friends, and Plummer always remembers how Tillman treated him and others. "He really had a special way of connecting with people. Anybody. When he would sit down with you, he was genuine and authentic. He called me before he left for his last deployment to check on me after I had gone through a pretty monumental change. He was calling to check on me to see how I was doing." We should all have a friend like Pat Tillman in our lives, or be that friend to others.

If you approach your life with passion, and are truly concerned about others and want to help them any way you can, you're mirroring Pat Tillman and who he was as a person. And there isn't a higher form of respect for somebody than trying to emulate how they lived.

- Was born in San Jose, California on November 6th, 1976.

- Had two younger brothers, Kevin Tillman and Richard Tillman.

- Turned down a big contract to go serve in the armed forces.

- Pat served in the United States Army as part of the 75th Ranger Regiment.

- Pat was drafted in the 7th round of the 1998 NFL Draft by the Arizona Cardinals.

- Set a Cardinals record for tackles in 2000 with 244.

- Inducted into the College Football Hall of Fame in 2010.

- The Arizona Cardinals retired his #40 to honor him after he passed away.

- Was married to his high school sweetheart Marie (Ugendi) Tillman.

- Pat was named after his father, Patrick Daniel Tillman Sr.

1. What college did Pat Tillman play for?

2. What position did Pat play?

3. What number did Pat Tillman wear?

4. What Army rank was Pat Tillman?

5. What motivated Pat Tillman to enlist in the Army?

6. True or False: Pat Tillman was the only one in his family who served in the military.

7. Where did Pat Tillman serve?

8. True or False: There is an autobiography on Pat Tillman that he wrote himself.

9. True or False: Pat Tillman supported the Iraq War.

10. True or False: Pat was a deeply religious man.

ANSWER

1. He played football for the Arizona State Sun Devils from 1994-1997.
2. In college he played linebacker, but in the NFL he played safety since he was smaller than the typical NFL linebacker. But he was a hard hitter!
3. He wore #42 when he played linebacker at Arizona State, and #40 when he played safety for the Cardinals.
4. Corporal
5. September 11th attacks.
6. False. The Tillman has a long history of military service to this country.
7. He served tours of duty in Afghanistan as well as Iraq.
8. False. There are several books on Pat Tillman, but he didn't write one before he passed away.
9. False. He didn't support the Iraq War. He felt we should be looking for Osama Bin Laden in Afghanistan, since Bin Laden was responsible for the 9/11 attacks. Pat deeply disagreed with being sent to fight in Iraq.
10. False. Pat was an atheist. He didn't believe in any religion. But he did believe in doing the right thing, standing up for others who needed his help, and defending the country. He was very patriotic and kind to those he cared about.

"Somewhere inside, we hear a voice. It leads us in the direction of the person we wish to become. But it is up to us whether or not to follow."

"Passion is what makes life interesting, what ignites our soul, fuels our love and carries our friendships, stimulates our intellect, and pushes our limits... A passion for life is contagious and uplifting. Passion cuts both ways... Those that make you feel on top of the world are equally able to turn it upside down... In my life I want to create passion in my own life and with those I care for. I want to feel, experience and live every emotion. I will suffer through the bad for the heights of the good."

"Passion is kind of an important word for me, whether it's playing sports or whether it's just living or whatever you're going to do. In my opinion you should be passionate about it or else, why do it?"

"Pat was a serious listener. He was one of the first people who really challenged my ideas: 'Do you really believe that? Why? Don't accept everything you read. You should question it all, take what makes sense, and throw away the rest.'" -Jon Krakauer

"To err on the side of passion is human and right, and the only way I'll live."

LESSONS FROM THE STORY

- Be a genuine friend to other people.

- Approach everything you do in your life with passion.

- Challenge your own thinking and ideas as you grow older.

- Speak up and do the right thing, even if no one else is doing it.

- Be humble in victory and gracious in defeat.

DERRICK THOMAS

KANSAS CITY'S GENTLE GIANT

If you ask anyone who saw Derrick Thomas play to describe him, you'll probably get several scary adjectives: fearsome, relentless, lightning fast, a quarterback's worst nightmare. And if they were talking about his time on the football field for the Chiefs from 1989 to 1999, they would be absolutely correct.

Thomas was a monster on the field as a cross between a linebacker and defensive end. At 6'3" and 255 pounds, he was a mountain of a man for anyone to try and block when he came after their team's quarterback. If anyone did manage to get a hand on him, they couldn't sustain their blocks. And if you were an offensive lineman who missed him entirely? Forget about it.

Your quarterback would be picking dirt out of his facemask two or three seconds later! In his 11 seasons in Kansas City, Thomas was a nine-time Pro Bowler, and racked up an astounding 126.5 sacks, good for 17th of all time on the NFL sack list.

As scary as he was to NFL quarterbacks, he had a softer side to him when he wasn't playing football. Thomas was known around Kansas City for being kind and down to earth toward fans, as well as for doing a lot of charitable and philanthropic work to help others who needed it the most. He grew up in a poor neighborhood in Miami, and knew what it was like to struggle with life early on. And once he made it as Kansas City's dominant pass rusher and defensive leader in the 1990s, he gave back any way he could to the kids who lived in his adopted home city.

The judge who had helped Derrick Thomas find the right path in life when he was struggling with staying out of trouble, was one of the people who helped him launch the Third and Long Foundation. The foundation enrolls 58 Kansas City kids per year in a literacy program to help them sharpen their reading skills.

While he played for the Chiefs, Thomas would meet the chosen kids in person the day before Kansas City home games at a local library in the city and read books to them. He would even sometimes invite opposing players to join him in reading books to the kids as well. He got such joy out of doing this, because he saw himself in those young kids. They were in the situation he used to be in when he was their age. And he knew if he could help them make it out, they'd find their dreams too.

The Third and Long Foundation might have been Derrick Thomas's pride and joy, but he eventually caught the eye of the most powerful man in the world for the work he was doing. President George H. W. Bush named the foundation as one of his Thousand Points of Light in 1992.

The President's Thousand Points of Light campaign was a movement to support any kind of volunteer work that helped children and communities all over the country, and Derrick Thomas earned national recognition for doing just that. He also received recognition from the NFL for his work, and was named the 1993 NFL Man of the Year as well.

But unlike many people, who would probably want to take credit for doing great things like that, that wasn't Derrick Thomas's way. Former Chiefs General Manager Carl Peterson, who drafted Thomas fourth overall in 1989, said he was always quick to avoid the spotlight when doing charity work for others. "All the charitable work he did, a lot was never publicized. He didn't want it that way," Peterson said.

Along with his charity work, there were also times when Thomas visited sick kids in person, and genuinely spent time with them and got to know them. Perhaps the most touching example of this, was when he visited Philip Tepe, a young basketball player. Tepe was also a hemophiliac, which meant that his blood didn't clot like everyone else's. He might only get a minor cut or scrape and he would still be at risk of bleeding severely. But he had also secretly been HIV positive since he was four years old. Once Tepe said that he had the disease, schools in his area in Oklahoma refused to play his team. Ignorance and fear caused people to shun him. It was the early 1990s at the time, and the world still knew very little about HIV and AIDS.

But this ignorance bothered Derrick Thomas. So he chartered a flight to Oklahoma to visit Tepe, and the two played video games together, and Thomas also gave Tepe the jersey he had worn during his very first Pro Bowl.

Two days later, Tepe passed away at 15 years old. But Derrick Thomas made sure that his last days were happy. This wasn't a football superstar meeting a fan and signing an autograph for them; this was simply a man making a new friend and visiting someone in need. That's the kind of person Derrick Thomas was.

Thomas was also beloved by his teammates and the Kansas City community. He also had a habit of being late for almost everything everywhere he went. Whether it was team meetings, or missing something else on a jam-packed schedule, he was often left scrambling to get to where he needed to go. And this habit would have tragic consequences on January 23, 2000.

Thomas and two of his friends were late for a flight from Kansas City to St. Louis. They were headed to watch the Rams play the Buccaneers in the NFC Championship Game, since the Chiefs were eliminated from the Playoffs. But Thomas was speeding along the highway even through the snow and ice from a massive blizzard that hit Kansas City earlier. Thomas went off the road and crashed, which threw him from his car, where he suffered a spinal injury that paralyzed him from the chest down. Two weeks later, he died at the age of 33 from a blood clot in his lungs.

But even with his tragic passing, Thomas's legacy is still felt today through the people he helped while he was alive, and through the Third and Long Foundation's work. Third and Long still strives to help Kansas City kids learn how to read, even after the organization was founded 34 years ago.

There was even a school named The Derrick Thomas Academy, which opened in September 2001, and served 1,000 students until it was closed in 2013.

For as terrifying as Derrick Thomas was to opposing quarterbacks, he was such a light to everyone else. One simple quote shows who he was at his core: "I think it's important for me to try to strive to make it to Canton, Ohio. But I think it's

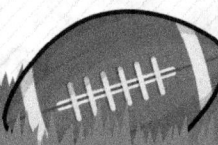

more important on my way there, to help and touch as many people as I possibly can."

Thomas made both of those things a reality, even though he never got to see the day he would be enshrined as a Pro Football Hall of Famer. He was inducted as part of the Class of 2009. He was a big man who played a ferocious style of football. But beyond that, he was a gentle giant with an even bigger heart for those in need.

Derrick Thomas spent his life serving others. How do you serve others in your life? Is there a food bank in your local town or city? Is there a homeless shelter in your area that you can donate to, or do volunteer work for? Can you help children who go to your local library by donating books or reading to them? All of these things were near and dear to Derrick Thomas's heart.

The world is sometimes a confusing and scary place. But there are always people who serve as lights to the rest of us. They inspire us to live better lives by their example. It costs nothing to be a good person other than simply caring more about others than yourself. Be a light for others by helping them when they need it the most. Be a Derrick Thomas!

- Set the all-time Alabama record for sacks in a single season with 27 in his senior year in 1988.

- Led the league in sacks in 1990 with 20. It's extremely rare for a defensive player to rack up that many sacks in one season, even if they're one of the best in the NFL like Thomas was.

- Derrick Thomas set the NFL single-game sack record when he sacked Seattle Seahawks quarterback Dave Krieg seven times. Unfortunately for Thomas and the Chiefs, they lost that game.

- Played his entire career from 1989-1999 with the Chiefs.

- Made the Pro Bowl nine straight times from 1989 to 1997.

- His nickname was simply "DT."

- His father, Robert Thomas, was a Captain in the Air Force.

- Derrick Thomas had seven children!

- He was inducted into the Pro Football Hall of Fame in 2009, and into the College Football Hall of Fame in 2014.

1. What number did Derrick Thomas wear when he played for the Chiefs?

2. True or false: Derrick Thomas had over 100 career sacks.

3. True or False: Derrick Thomas is in the Top 20 in NFL history for sacks.

4. How big was Derrick Thomas?

5. True or False: Derrick Thomas grew up in Kansas City.

6. True or False: Derrick got in trouble with the law as a kid.

7. True or False: Derrick Thomas only ever played linebacker at any level.

8. True or False: Derrick Thomas set the single-season sack record for Alabama football when he was in college.

9. True or False: Derrick was taken fourth overall in the 1989 Draft.

10. True or False: When he wasn't sacking quarterbacks on the field, Derrick Thomas loved to spend his time at local libraries in Kansas City reading to little kids.

ANSWER

1. #58.
2. True! He had 126.5 career sacks.
3. True! Derrick Thomas is 17th on the all-time career sacks list.
4. He was huge! He stood at 6'3 and weighed 255 pounds!
5. False. He grew up in South Miami.
6. True. And he was sent to the Dade Marine Institute, where teachers straightened him out. He turned his life around from that point onward.
7. False. When he was in high school, he played as a tight end and running back.
8. True! He racked up an eye-popping 18 sacks his junior season!
9. True!
10. True! Even though he was a nightmare for opposing quarterbacks, he had a softer side, and loved to help out little kids any way he could!

"On the field accolades are great, but in order to reach your full potential, you have to overstep the boundaries of football and go out into the community and be an All-Pro there too."

"I don't ever want it to be a question whether I'm a Pro Bowl-caliber player, I believe I'm the best at what I do, and it's my responsibility to play like I'm capable of playing and help this defense as much as possible."

"Whenever I see those crimson jerseys and crimson helmets, I feel humbled to have played football for Alabama. Other players in the NFL talk to me about their schools and their traditions. I just smile knowing the immense love Alabama fans have for our school and its football program. I'm proud to be a part of that Crimson Tide heritage."

"I looked at him as one of the finest people I've been around. The one thing I'll always remember is the smile. That's one thing I'll never get out of my mind. I just know this: Derrick will hang over this stadium forever. After every game, he'd walk across the field with a smile on his face, not because the Chiefs won, but because that's what he was. That's how I'll always remember him." -Gunther Cunningham

"As much as he was Derrick Thomas the football player, I mean Derrick Thomas the dad was, you know, who I remember him as. It was important for me to kind of be around the people who have been a part of my life throughout this whole thing and just kind of celebrate what he meant to Kansas City." -Derrion Thomas

LESSONS FROM THE STORY

- Show kindness to others. Especially those who are down on their luck and cannot help themselves.

- It's always worth it to make a positive impact in the life of a child.

- If you can, do good things for other people in secret. Don't draw attention to yourself.

- Make sure you're on time to important things. Don't run late if you can help it.

- Try to spend your whole life doing kind things for others, so you can leave a legacy in the future.

BONUS

Unlock an exclusive treasure trove of football knowledge with our bonus content: 100 Unique Football Facts and Trivia Questions. This special collection will enrich your understanding of the game and provide you with captivating trivia to impress friends and family. From iconic moments in football history to intriguing facts about legendary players, this content is perfect for deepening your appreciation of the sport. Enhance your journey with these fascinating insights and become a true football aficionado. Whether you're a lifelong fan or new to the game, this bonus content will provide hours of enjoyment. Get ready to explore the wonders of football like never before.

To access your bonus content, simply scan the QR code below with your smartphone and dive into the world of football!

BRETT FAVRE

#4 WINS ONE FOR HIS DAD

Brett Favre is one of the greatest quarterbacks in NFL history. If you look up the definition of the word "gunslinger" in the dictionary, you might just see his picture. He is a Hall of Famer, Super Bowl Champion, three-time NFL MVP, 11-time Pro Bowler, and he's thrown for over 71,000 yards and 508 touchdowns. But for all of his accomplishments, arguably his most inspiring performance on a football field wasn't in the playoffs or the Super Bowl, it was when he was dealing with one of the greatest tragedies of his life.

On December 21, 2003, Brett's father Irv Favre had a heart attack while driving near Kiln, Mississippi, Brett's hometown. Irv ended up in a ditch, and was pronounced dead shortly thereafter. He was only 58 years old.

Not only was Irv's death a tragic loss for Brett and the rest of the Favre family, but it was also a loss that was deeply felt by the people of Kiln, Mississippi. Irv Favre was a well-respected figure in the tiny town of just over 2,200 people. He was a beloved teacher like his wife, Bonita, Brett's mother.

Irv was also the high school football coach for several years, and coached Brett while he was a quarterback at Hancock North Central High School. But now, after Brett had played seemingly every game for Green Bay since joining the team in 1992 after being traded from the Falcons, he had a decision to make: Play the night after Irv died, or mourn his father and take a week off.

Many people would understandably take time off work if a parent suddenly passed away. Losing a parent or loved one is an absolutely tragic thing. But for Brett, it wasn't even a question. In an interview with broadcaster Cris Collinsworth, he said he wanted to play to honor his dad. He didn't even give it a second thought. But at the same time, he still understood how much he was hurting, and he knew how big the game would be for him. "You always want to play great. But there's an elevated sense of 'I really want to do this for them.' That's a lot of pressure, I'll be honest with you. I've played in a lot of games. By far, the most pressure I've ever felt to perform, was that night."

Not only did Brett feel the pressure of trying to play his best game to honor Irv, but there was also added pressure on him to continue playing well for his teammates. At the time, Green Bay was 8-6, and trying to win for their fifth time in seven games to stay alive in the playoff hunt and NFC North race. But he was ready to step up to the challenge. Bret may have been brokenhearted over the death of his dad. But there was a fire burning inside him to play his best football. And the poor, unfortunate team that was in his way was the Oakland Raiders.

And on December 22, 2003, with millions watching him around the world on Monday Night Football, Favre put on a show for the ages. He was already a fantastic quarterback. But the adrenaline and emotion of playing for his dad in front of a worldwide audience just cranked up Brett Favre's abilities to levels that were off the charts!

Brett Favre was normally a hit or miss kind of quarterback. Yes, he scored a bunch of touchdowns in his career. But he also threw a lot of interceptions because he was always trying to push the ball downfield and make the big play. He could live with the mistakes. That was his style. He was go big or go home.

But on that night, Favre wasn't just a playmaker; he was also incredibly mobile and accurate. The best quarterbacks can sense when they make good throws. And their best throws have pinpoint accuracy. They make sure to throw the football exactly to where their receivers can come down with it, while also keeping it just out of reach of the defensive backs. And on the biggest stage in what he considered the toughest game of his career, Brett Favre played arguably the best game of his life. He went 22-30 for 400 yards, four touchdowns and zero interceptions.

Not only that, but his play seemed to raise the level of his teammates. They were rallying around their leader. They knew he was badly hurt emotionally, and struggling with the pain of losing his dad. But they seemed to play harder and better than usual. The offensive linemen gave him all the time in the world to throw. The wide receivers were seemingly wide open all the time. The running backs ran harder than normal. And the defensive linemen seemed more aggressive than usual, sacking Oakland quarterback Rick Mirer three times.

When the smoke had cleared, the Packers didn't just beat the Raiders. They absolutely destroyed Oakland by a final score of 41-7. Brett Favre had done it. He had lived up to the goals he had set for himself just hours earlier. He helped Green Bay win a critical game that would eventually clinch the NFC North Championship and a playoff berth.

But most importantly, he knew he had made his dad proud. Brett was really struggling in his faith after Irv had died. And in the interview with Cris Collinsworth, Tom Brady, Bill Belichick years after the game, Favre attributed how well he played in the game to divine intervention.

"I talked about it after the game, divine intervention. I really didn't know exactly what that meant until most recently as I thought about it. Like most people I thought, 'God, just show yourself. I need to know if you're real.' What happened was, I believe, is that was the sign I was looking for. It has made it easier. Because I know he's up there, and he's proud. And what a way to honor him."

Brett played his absolute best with his given gifts despite the awful tragedy he'd been through just a day before the greatest game of his career. Most people would have given up or taken time off to heal in that situation. But he used the game to honor his father.

You're still young enough that you may be fortunate to have one or both parents. And hopefully you have both sets of grandparents as well. Treasure and honor them all for as long as you have them. You'll miss them one day.

For those of you who have lost parents or grandparents, do you honor them with how you live? Do you have things that you remember them by? Brett Favre honored his dad while he was alive with how he played football. He was born the son of a head coach. And he honored his dad after he passed away by playing his best game.

Think back to the last time you honored your parents or grandparents, whether they're still with you or not. Maybe you baked or cooked with your mom or grandma. Maybe you fished with your dad or grandpa. Or perhaps you remember them when you eat a certain food, or when a certain song comes on the radio. I know I occasionally drink a Diet Coke in honor of my grandfather who passed away, and it always makes me smile. And my grandmother on my mother's side always loved big family gatherings during the holidays when she was here. It always makes me happy to spend time with family during Thanksgiving or Christmas, because I know it makes her happy.

Always look for ways to honor your family. And if some of them are gone, use your happy memories of them to heal, and to live your best life. Or use what they've taught you to inspire everyone else around you. Irv Favre taught his son Brett how to play football and be a great quarterback and teammate. But he also taught Brett how to persevere, fight, and succeed during the most difficult time in his life.

Take a cue from Brett Favre and honor your parents and grandparents in the best way you know how. Appreciate them and spend time with them while they're here. And remember and honor them if they're not. Either way, it would make them smile with pride, knowing that you've remembered everything they taught you!

- Brett Favre was born on October 10th, 1969 in Gulfport, Mississippi.

- He's the son of Irvin Favre and Bonita Favre.

- Irv was the football coach for Hancock North Central High School.

- Brett played college football for the Southern Mississippi Golden Eagles football team from 1987-1990.

- Southern Miss wanted Brett to play as a defensive back. But he wanted to play quarterback. So he started all the way down the depth chart as the team's seventh string quarterback!

- He's an 11-time Pro Bowler.

- He's also a three-time NFL MVP

- He led the Packers to a win in Super Bowl 31 against the New England Patriots.

- He has the most consecutive starts in NFL history at 321 games in a row.

- He's tied for the longest pass play in NFL history, 99 yards!

1. True or False: Brett Favre holds the NFL record for career interceptions.

2. How many interceptions has he thrown in his career?

3. True or False: Brett Favre has over 71,000 career passing yards.

4. True or False: The Packers drafted Brett Favre in 1991.

5. True or False: Brett Favre's first career pass was an interception returned for a touchdown (a pick six).

6. How many teams did Brett Favre play for in his NFL career?

7. Brett Favre has a cool nickname. What is it?

8. How did he earn his nickname?

9. When was Brett Favre inducted into the Pro Football Hall of Fame?

10. True or False: Off the field, Brett Favre is often known for his charity work.

ANSWER

1. *True!*
2. *336 interceptions.*
3. *True! He has a total of 71,838 career passing yards.*
4. *False. The Atlanta Falcons took Favre with the 33rd overall pick.*
5. *True!*
6. *Four teams (Falcons, Packers, Jets, Vikings).*
7. *The Gunslinger.*
8. *Brett Favre is nicknamed The Gunslinger because of being raised in the South, and because he wasn't afraid to take risks and be gutsy, just like a real gunslinger or gunfighter in the days of the Wild West!*
9. *2016.*
10. *True! He works with many charitable organizations, with the Make a Wish Foundation being a big one.*

"You have to believe you're great. You have to have an air about you. My success wasn't because I was a great talent, but because I wanted it more than anybody else. Every minute I step on that field, I want to prove I'm the best player in the league."

"Most talented players don't always succeed. Some don't even make the team. It's more about what's inside."

"If I were to make a list, I would include the interceptions, the sacks, the really painful losses. Those times when I've been down, when I've been kicked around, I hold on to those. In a way those are the best times I've ever had, because that's when I've found out who I am. And what I want to be."

"It's all about chemistry. Talent alone won't get it done."

"I love doing what I do."

LESSONS FROM THE STORY

- Deal with your losses, but don't dwell on them. The people who love you wouldn't want that.

- True champions rise to the occasion.

- Leaders can rally their teammates and raise their level of performance.

- Honor your departed loved ones by living your life in a way that would make them happy.

- Honor them by remembering all the stuff they enjoyed in this life, and doing it for them

KURT WARNER

FAITH THROUGH ADVERSITY

Everyone in life goes through some kind of trouble at some point or another. But how we handle those times end up shaping us into who we eventually become. Many people also find ways to cope with life, and outlets to channel their energy. Some outlets aren't helpful like drugs or alcohol or getting in trouble with the law. But for Hall of Fame quarterback Kurt Warner, his outlet for getting through hard times was football. But before he ever became a successful quarterback and one of the all-time greats, he leaned on his faith as a Christian to help him make it through the storms of life.

Coming out of college, Warner wasn't a star; he wasn't even on anybody's radar. He went undrafted and rode the bench for the first three years of his career. But in his senior season with the Northern Iowa Panthers in 1993, he went 8-4 as a starter, and threw over for over 2,700 yards and 17 touchdowns.

This was good enough to get a tryout with the Green Bay Packers the next year, but he had almost no chance of being the starting quarterback. He was competing against Hall of Famer Brett Favre, seasoned pro Mark Brunell, and Heisman Winner Ty Detmer. The odds were stacked heavily against him, and he unfortunately did not make it. On top of that, he was struggling to make ends meet to support his wife and their two kids at the time. He was only making $5.50 an hour stocking shelves at a local grocery store, working as an assistant football coach at Northern Iowa, and living in his parents' basement.

His football dreams had stalled out—he had hit rock bottom. However, he never lost the itch to play the sport he loved, and a relatively new football league at the time called the Arena Football League would be the next door opened for him on his journey.

While in the AFL, Warner really got his chance to shine. In 1996 and 1997, he led the Iowa Barnstormers, a team based in Des Moines, Iowa, only two hours away from where he grew up, to back-to-back Arena Bowl appearances for the first time in the team's history! Even though he failed to win either championship game, in his three seasons with the Barnstormers, Warner threw for over 10,000 yards, 183 touchdowns, and just 43 interceptions.

He was no longer at rock bottom. His star was rising; he just didn't know it yet. And he'd soon catch the eye of Rams coach Dick Vermeil. Warner signed a contract with the team, but he had one more step to take before he was in line for a shot at the big time. He was sent to the Netherlands to play for the Amsterdam Admirals in NFL Europe. Just like he did in the

Arena Football League, Warner lit it up as the Admirals quarterback, leading NFL Europe in passing yards and touchdowns that season.

More importantly, playing in Europe showed Kurt's dedication to chasing his lifelong dream of becoming a starting quarterback in the NFL. It didn't matter where he played football, or for whom, he was going to make his dream happen. This was a dream he'd had ever since he was a boy growing up in Burlington, Iowa. Ever since he'd watched Dan Marino and the Dolphins battle Joe Montana and the 49ers in Super Bowl 19 as a kid, he had that dream in his sights. And now here it was, so close to him but so far.

It's always unfortunate when someone gets hurt. But a preseason injury to the Rams' projected starting quarterback Trent Green, provided the opening Kurt Warner needed to realize his dream. He had made it. Five years after he had been living with his wife and kids in his parents' basement, and making $5.50 an hour as a grocery store clerk, he had a job that only 30 other people in the entire world had. And once he had that dream finally in his grasp, he took it and ran with it!

Most of the time when an NFL quarterback starts their career, they usually struggle as a rookie or even a second-year player before coming into their own. The game is faster, guys hit harder, and everyone is the best in the world at what they do. But thanks to his years as a gunslinger in the Arena Football League and NFL Europe, Kurt Warner took the NFL world by storm!

In 1999, under seasoned head coach Dick Vermeil, offensive coordinator Mike Martz and with teammates like Marshall Faulk, Isaac Bruce, and Torry Holt, Warner and the Rams blasted off like a rocket ship! Their high-flying offense led the NFL in multiple categories including points per game (33), yards per game (400), and passing yards per game (272). Their defense was just as dangerous too, holding teams to an average of 74 rushing yards per game, and averaging 3.5 sacks per game. They were a complete team. They rolled through the regular season with a 13-3 record, and the top seed in the NFC for the Playoffs!

Once they were in the Playoffs, the Rams had to win their games in several different ways. They couldn't steamroll everybody like they had done all year. They survived a tough rally by the Minnesota Vikings to win in the Divisional Round in a shootout, 49-37, and won the NFC Championship against the Tampa Bay Buccaneers 11-6, in one of the lowest-scoring playoff games in history to advance to Super Bowl 34 against the Tennessee Titans! In the big game, Kurt Warner and the Rams staked themselves to a 16-0 lead in the third quarter. But Tennessee refused to go away quietly, as the Titans shredded St. Louis' defense later in the game to tie it up at 16 all.

There are few situations in life that are more helpless, than being a star quarterback who can't do anything other than watch on the sidelines, as a Super Bowl Championship potentially slips away. Kurt Warner had one of the best games of his life up to that point. But the Rams' offensive attack had stalled, while the Titans gained new life. Fortunately for Warner and the Rams, there was one big play left in the tank. And it turned out to be the go-ahead score that would end up winning the game. He heaved the ball deep to Isaac Bruce, who adjusted to catch the ball, made the Titans cornerback miss, and ran it all the way for a 73-yard touchdown to put St. Louis up 23-16!

Kurt Warner had done all he could do. He had finished his part in the game. He threw two touchdowns and 414 yards. But it would be on the shoulders of the Rams defense to bring home a World Championship. Titans quarterback Steve McNair marched Tennessee all the way down to the Rams 10-yard line on a 78-yard drive. They looked poised to tie the game with just seconds left. But on the final play, Rams linebacker Mike Jones tackled Titans receiver Kevin Dyson a yard short of scoring. Three feet. That was the margin of victory for the Rams.

One of the greatest Super Bowls in history was in the books. As Kurt Warner and Rams coach Dick Vermeil were hugging and in tears, confetti rained down on everybody at the Georgia Dome in Atlanta. But while confetti may have been coming down, Warner was focused on something and someone far above him, when he was asked by a reporter what was going through his mind on that game-winning touchdown pass: "Well, first thing's first. I've got to thank my Lord and Savior up above—thank you Jesus!"

Kurt Warner went through some truly hard times before he made it big. He was briefly homeless before he found his job as a grocery store clerk. He struggled to provide for himself, his wife, and their kids. He lost his in-laws to a tornado, the Packers cut him, and he had to work so hard just to even make the Rams depth chart as a third-string quarterback. He could have been bitter, angry, and impatient. But now he's a Hall of Fame quarterback. An unknown guy from Iowa is one of the greatest quarterbacks in NFL history!

You may be struggling through hard times in life. Sometimes, things might be so hopeless that you can't pull yourself up. But work as hard as you can. That's what Kurt Warner did. And it was the best decision he ever made!

- Born June 22nd 1971 in Burlington, Iowa.

- Stands 6'2 and weighs 214 pounds.

- Kurt Warner originally wanted to play defensive end or wide receiver in high school. He had no desire to play quarterback at that time.

- Along with being an NFL Hall of Famer, Kurt Warner is probably the most famous Arena Football League player of all time.

- Played for the Iowa Barnstormers from 1995-1997.

- A spider bite he suffered while on his honeymoon cost him a chance to try out for the Chicago Bears.

- Two-time MVP.

- Four-time Pro Bowler.

- Tied for the most touchdown passes in a single postseason.

- Threw the most complete passes in a row in NFL history.

1. What number did Kurt Warner wear for his entire NFL career?

2. True or False: Kurt Warner is in both the Arena Football Hall of Fame and the Pro Football Hall of Fame.

3. When was Kurt Warner inducted into the Pro Football Hall of Fame?

4. What was the nickname of the Rams teams of the 1990s?

5. Why were the teams nicknamed that?

6. True or False: Kurt Warner has won two Super Bowls.

7. Which team defeated Kurt Warner and the Rams to win the Super Bowl following the 2001 season?

8. How many NFL teams has Kurt Warner played for?

9. What religion is Kurt Warner?

10. True or False: Kurt Warner's wife, Brenda Warner, served in the United States Marines until 1990.

ANSWER

1. *Lucky number 13!*
2. *True!*
3. *2017.*
4. *The Greatest Show on Turf.*
5. *The Rams were often called The Greatest Show on Turf because of their high-scoring, fast-paced offense.*
6. *False. He won one Super Bowl with the Rams, and lost two.*
7. *The New England Patriots, led by a young Tom Brady, won their first Super Bowl in team history by defeating the Rams in Super Bowl 36.*
8. *He's played for the Packers, Rams, Giants and Cardinals.*
9. *He is a devout Christian, and he credits Jesus Christ with helping him out of his hard times in life before he found success.*
10. *True!*

"If you're willing to put yourself and your dreams on the line, at the very least you'll discover an inner strength you may not have known existed."

"I am where I am because I believed and I never gave up."

"Whether I'm a Super Bowl Champion or a regular guy stocking groceries at the Hy-Vee, sharing my faith and glorifying Jesus is the central focus of my time on this earth."

"I believe that the Lord has a plan for each of us that's better than anything we can imagine, even if that plan isn't obvious to us at every stage. He prepared me for this over a long period of time - in lower-profile locker rooms and the grocery store and in Europe, through all the personal tragedies and in spite of the people who doubted me along the way."

"No matter what happens on the football field it doesn't change the kind of person I am."

LESSONS FROM THE STORY

- You will face adversity in life as you go along. It's guaranteed. But it's how you handle it that matters the most.

- Family is everything!

- Keep going, even if it feels like you've hit rock bottom.

- Earlier experiences in life can set you up to succeed later on.

- No matter what life throws at you, don't become bitter and angry. Instead, embrace where you are, work hard, and wait patiently for the next opportunity to come.

13

CJ STROUD

FAITH AND FOOTBALL

Several of the world's greatest football players have used the sport to overcome personal challenges and tragedies in their lives. But for a few others, they've gone even further by leaning on their faith and spiritual connections too. There is probably nobody more relevant right now when it comes to this, than CJ Stroud, the rookie quarterback of the Houston Texans. Stroud played extremely well in his first season in the NFL, revitalizing a team that had only won three games in 2022. He threw for 23 touchdowns and only five interceptions, went 10-7 as a starter, and led Houston to their first playoff appearance and win since 2019. But before all his success, Stroud really struggled growing up in California.

For most of his childhood, Stroud had a good relationship with his parents. Especially his father, Coleridge. Stroud said several times that his dad was his best friend. Not only that, but Stroud's father also instilled Christian values and a genuine belief in Jesus in him from an early age since his dad was a pastor. But a dark, sad part of his dad's past would bring CJ's life crashing down.

Before he got clean and got his act together around the time CJ was born in 2001, Coleridge served a decade in prison on multiple felony charges. Everything was normal and happy for the Stroud family for many years. Until one sad night on April 12, 2015. By that time, Coleridge had sadly fallen into bad habits with drugs, and carjacked a woman while forcing him to drive her to a place to buy more drugs. After beating her up, Coleridge used her stolen car to outrun the police. He eventually crashed the car, and jumped into the San Diego Bay, where he was eventually arrested.

Because of California's three-strikes law when it comes to crime, CJ Stroud's dad was sentenced to 38 years in prison. He's currently doing his time in Folsom Prison near Sacramento. But not only did Coleridge's mistake end up landing him behind bars, it also put the Stroud family in a tough spot financially. CJ's mom Kim had to move CJ and his three siblings out of their home, and into a tiny apartment above the storage facility where she worked. They were on the brink of becoming homeless. But in the middle of all the stress and chaos going on around him, CJ focused on the one thing he knew how to do extremely well—play football.

Even though he couldn't afford to go to many football camps, and he sometimes played without regular cleats, which led to blisters on his feet, CJ did whatever it took to improve and get better as a player at Rancho Cucamonga High School. He even watched YouTube videos of his favorite quarterback,

Drew Brees, to help him figure out how to improve his footwork so he could throw more accurately.

All the hard work and hours of study eventually paid off for CJ, as he exploded during his senior year for the Rancho Cucamonga Cougars. He threw for over 3,800 yards, an eye-popping 47 touchdowns, and only nine interceptions. This was good enough to get him an invite to the Elite 11, a quarterback competition held at Nike world headquarters in Oregon. The competition is so famous and well-known that several current and former star quarterbacks in college and the NFL have participated in the past. This includes Matthew Stafford, Vince Young, Jameis Winston, Andrew Luck, Tim Tebow, Justin Fields, and many others.

CJ didn't just impress coaches and scouts at the 2019 version of the Elite 11; he was named the competition's MVP. This opened the floodgates, and college offers just started rolling in! He received offers from Colorado, Michigan, Georgia, and Ohio State. He ultimately chose to play for Ohio State, and led the Buckeyes as an athletic, hard-throwing quarterback. In 25 starts for the Buckeyes, Stroud went 21-4, threw for over 8,100 yards, 85 touchdowns, and just 12 interceptions over three seasons. He was incredibly accurate, loved by his teammates, and respected around the country.

While he unfortunately never won a National Championship with Ohio State, CJ still played well enough to be selected by a Houston Texans team that desperately needed a young leader to bring them back from rock bottom. And once the team selected him second overall, he would get his opportunity to show them what he could do. Hard work had lifted him from poverty. But someone else upstairs was ultimately guiding his path.

Even though he went through a lot of darkness to get to where he is right now, one constant in CJ Stroud's life is his

faith in Jesus Christ. Even though his father is currently in prison, Coleridge instilled CJ's faith and values in him, and his Christian outlook has helped him to stay grounded and humble. His faith has also enabled him to forgive his father, even though it wasn't easy for him.

"When I talk to him now, I don't hold any ill will," CJ said. "I told him 'I love you.' He's made his mistakes. I've made mine. It's not about the bad. It's the nature of the beast. You accept the good with the bad. I thank God for a second chance at this game."

And along with being able to make his football dreams come true as one of the new young stars of the NFL, CJ has also gotten a second chance at life in general. If his football dreams hadn't come true thanks to his faith in God as well as hard work, who knows where he would be today. He may still be living in that small apartment above the storage facility where his mother used to work.

But his new life is certainly a charmed one. He's been abundantly blessed in his new opportunity as the Texans' starting quarterback of the future. And instead of letting all his fame and good fortune go to his head, CJ still continues to stay humble. After every game, whether it's a win or loss, he continues to proclaim his faith in Jesus, and thanks him for the opportunity to simply keep playing at all.

CJ took that opportunity and ran with it. Even though the Texans were eventually defeated by the Baltimore Ravens in the playoffs to end their 2023 season, Stroud is all but a lock to win the 2023 Offensive Rookie of the Year Award.

But this is just the beginning of the young signal caller's journey. He put the rest of the league on notice in Year 1, and has the Texans poised to climb to even greater heights than just winning the AFC South or a playoff game over the Cleveland Browns. If he keeps climbing, so will his team. And maybe, just maybe, he'll lead Houston to their first Super Bowl Championship in team history!

But no matter what happens, CJ Stroud hasn't forgotten where he came from. He hasn't forgotten his parents or family. And he certainly hasn't forgotten his faith in Jesus Christ as the driving force behind where he is today.

There's a lot to learn from the story of CJ Stroud. But the three main lessons he can teach you are these:

1. If you want a dream bad enough, no one will outwork you.
2. Family is everything.
3. Faith during dark times in life can get you through whatever you struggle with.

It's always easy to watch CJ Stroud, or some other amazing athlete make highlight-reel plays. But we often forget what these people had to go through to get where they are today. We only see the successful results of their struggle.

If you are working toward a dream or goal right now, keep going. Keep working at it even when it's hard. And trust in your family, or the people you consider family, to have your back. Everyone needs a support system, no matter what dream they're chasing after.

And lastly, have faith. Just work hard, stay humble, and your dreams will become a reality. CJ Stroud did that, and is now living his best life. You can live yours too!

- Born in Rancho Cucamonga, California on October 3rd, 2001

- His mom nicknamed him Cool Breeze since Stroud has always been level-headed and calm.

- His real first name, Coleridge, comes from a British Composer. named Samuel Taylor Coleridge. The name was originally given to his great grandfather, and then passed down each generation until it became his. So CJ Stroud's real name is Coleridge Bernard Stroud IV.

- Threw for 573 yards against Utah in the 2022 Rose Bowl, which is a single-game Ohio State record.

- He went 21-4 as the starting quarterback at Ohio State. Impressive!

- He was a Heisman finalist twice during his Ohio State career.

- He was taken #2 overall in the 2023 NFL Draft.

- He earned 2023 NFL Offensive Rookie of the Year honors.

- He was also named to his first Pro Bowl following the 2023 regular season.

- He became the youngest starting quarterback to win a playoff game at 22 years, 102 days.

1. True or False: CJ Stroud and his family were once very nearly homeless before he became a football superstar.

2. How far could CJ throw the football at just nine years old?

3. True or False: CJ Stroud is the highest Ohio State quarterback ever taken in the Draft.

4. True or False: CJ didn't even begin playing football until his junior year in high school.

5. What was the name of the famous quarterback tournament that CJ attended in high school?

6. True or False: CJ lost the tournament.

7. Which schools offered scholarships to CJ?

8. True or False: CJ Stroud is not religious or spiritual at all.

9. True or False: CJ is great friends with Panthers starting quarterback Bryce Young.

10. True or False: CJ Stroud currently has a passer rating over 100.

ANSWER

1. True.
2. 50 yards!
3. True.
4. True.
5. Elite 11
6. False! He won the tournament, and was actually the 2019 Elite 11 MVP!
7. Ohio State, Georgia, Michigan, Oregon, Baylor, Washington State, Utah and Colorado all offered scholarships to CJ after the Elite 11 Tournament.
8. False. He's a devout Christian who credits Jesus with getting him to where he currently is.
9. True! The two have been friends since high school, and were selected with the first two picks of the 2023 NFL Draft. Young went #1, and Stroud went #2.
10. True! He's lighting it up!

"I want to be known as the best. No one can question my heart. I don't think anybody could question how hard I tried to win this game. I left everything on the table. There was no rock I didn't flip over. Nothing I could've done more, other than play better today. But it's not like I left it to chance." -CJ after Ohio State lost to Michigan in 2022.

"Honestly, I try to help people, not just with money. When you just give somebody $500, you just open them up to your pockets, you're not giving them a real chance at life. I think it's about setting people up."

"DeMeco Ryans is the perfect guy for the job. He brings something out of his players, and it's indescribable."

"When I talk to him now, I don't hold any ill will," he told The Pivot. "I told him, 'I love you.' He made his mistakes. I've made mine. It's not about the bad." -CJ on his current relationship with his father.

"God was trying to teach me to sit down, teach me perseverance and to just wait."

LESSONS FROM THE STORY

- Nobody can outwork you if you have a great work ethic.

- Being there for family is everything, even if they struggle.

- Faith in God can get you through rough times.

- You can make something of yourself in life, no matter where you come from.

- Even if things don't go your way, don't get mad or angry at the world.

14

MICHAEL IRVIN

KEEPING THE PROMISE

On the outside, Michael Irvin embodied what it meant to be a Dallas Cowboy when he played in the late 1980s and in the 1990s. He was the face of the franchise. He was loud and cocky. He knew how good he was as a wide receiver, and if you were playing against him, he wasn't afraid to tell you about it. Even on the rare chance that you actually got the better of him on gameday, he would still talk smack. But that confidence and swagger was there for a reason, and it was born out of a tragedy that occurred early in his life.

Michael grew up in a small, cramped home in Fort Lauderdale, Florida. It was just a small, three-bedroom house. But it was supposed to somehow hold him, his dad Walter,

mom Pearl, and his 16 brothers and sisters. But just before Michael was set to play football his senior season, his dad passed away from cancer. Before Walter Irvin died, he had one last talk with Michael. What his dad told him next would drive him for the rest of his life, both on and off the football field: "Son, I feel I'm going home on the morning train. I want you to promise me you'll always take care of your mom. I'm so proud of you."

Immediately after the loss of his father, Michael ran straight to St. Thomas Aquinas High School, even though it was six or seven miles away from the hospital. And even though he eventually stopped running once he got to the school, and his mom and football coach found him near the field, in some ways, his running has never stopped.

After the death of his father, Michael wanted to get a job to help support his mother and siblings. But Pearl Irvin knew her son had something special inside him. She knew he was meant for more than just working every day at some normal job. And so, she encouraged and supported his desire to play football. And he took that dream and ran with it. Right to the University of Miami, an hour away from where he lived. Football was going to be his way of getting his family out of poverty. And it would be his way of keeping his promise to his father.

When Michael Irvin began playing college football for Miami in 1984, the Hurricanes were fresh off their first National Championship win in 1983 over Nebraska. There was a swagger to the team that wasn't there before coach Howard Schnellenberger had arrived. And all Michael did was add to it.

The Miami Hurricanes quickly became the "bad boys" of college football. They would run up the score on opponents when they could, they would talk trash, and they would often be incredibly physical with opponents. Michael was one of them.

He would often talk trash with opposing cornerbacks trying to slow him down or stop him. And after he scored a touchdown, he would always dance and then point his fingers to the sky. But even though his haters didn't like him showing off, every time he pointed to the sky, it was in honor of, and in tribute to his father Walter Irvin. He was using his abilities on the football field to make Walter proud. But Michael's promise to his dad hadn't come true yet. The fulfillment of his promise wouldn't start to take shape until 1988, when he was drafted by the Dallas Cowboys #11 overall at just 22 years old.

The Cowboys were a bad team when Michael Irvin arrived in Big D. From a football standpoint, Dallas was awful during Irvin's rookie season. The team won just three games, and legendary head coach Tom Landry was fired by Dallas owner Jerry Jones. A score of 3-13 was a far cry from the success that Dallas was used to under Tom Landry. Landry had won a pair of Super Bowls with the Cowboys in 1971 and 1977. But by 1988, he had worn out his welcome. Replacing Landry would be none other than Michael Irvin's old coach from the University of Miami, Jimmy Johnson.

But things wouldn't immediately get better. In fact, they would actually get worse. In 1989, Dallas dropped to just 1-15. This was rock bottom. But several players would spark the Cowboys' run back to the top, like quarterback Troy Aikman, running back Emmitt Smith, and Michael Irvin himself.

In 1991, two years after recovering from blowing out his knee, Michael Irvin would have his first truly great season. He lit up the scoreboard and put the rest of the league on notice, as he hauled in 93 catches for over 1,500 yards and eight touchdowns! And in 1992, Irvin would help lead the Cowboys to somewhere they hadn't been since 1977: the Super Bowl. And Dallas wouldn't just win, they would smoke the Buffalo Bills 52-17! Michael Irvin certainly played his part too, as he caught six passes for 114 yards and two touchdowns.

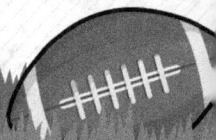

Years later, when he was asked what it was like playing in his very first Super Bowl, Irvin struggled to put it into words: "There was nothing like it. That was the first Super Bowl. Everybody always asks which one's better. There's nothing like the first. And it was in Hollywood. That was the last time we had a Super Bowl in LA."

However, Michael wouldn't get to experience what it felt like to win a Championship just once; he experienced it two more times in 1993 and 1995 as well. The Cowboys were the team of the 1990s. And a big reason for that was thanks to #88. The Playmaker. Michael Irvin was instrumental in their dominant run. He was a key piece in bringing a down and out Cowboys team back to the top of the football world.

Even more special to Michael than Dallas's wins in the big game, was his ability to keep his promise to his father Walter Irvin in 1983, to take care of his mother and the rest of the family. In his speech following his 2007 induction into the Pro Football Hall of Fame, Michael honored his mother and his aunt Fannie, her older sister.

"My mom and my aunt Fannie, her older sister, they are part of my travel squad now. And as we travel, all they want is a nice room and an open tab on room service. And when my workday is done, I get to come by their room. We tell stories, we laugh and we have fun. And we always end the night with them telling me, 'Baby, this is what God meant when he said our latter days will be better than our former days.' I can't tell you how it makes me feel to know that God uses me to deliver his promise. I love you, mom. I love you, aunt Fanny."

How do you honor your parents? There are many different ways to do that. Helping around the house with chores when they ask, respecting them without talking back, and letting your parents and others know how much they mean to you, are all ways you can honor them.

Reflect on the best qualities of your parents too. Perhaps your mom has been kind, loving and gentle to you as you're growing up. Perhaps your father has shown you what it means to be strong, and how to dig deep, roll up your sleeves and work hard.

And even for those of you who might not have biological or adoptive fathers and mothers, who are the people who are your "father figures" and "mother figures" in your life? They have all played an important role in shaping how you've grown up so far, and will continue to do that for you until their time is done on earth.

What promises have you made to them? Are you keeping them? If you're struggling to keep them right now, that's okay. Let Michael Irvin's promise to his dad be a gentle reminder and inspiration for you. Without good parents, or people willing to step up in our lives, we have no sense of direction.

Good parents are extremely important for shaping us into who we eventually become as people. And they love us more than anyone else on earth. Michael Irvin proved that by keeping his promise to his parents.

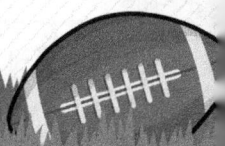

- Michael Irvin was born in Fort Lauderdale, Florida on March 5th, 1966.

- He is the 15th of 17 children in his family. Huge family!

- Along with Emmitt Smith and Troy Aikman, Michael Irvin was one of the players nicknamed "The Triplets." All three of them were responsible for Dallas' explosive offense during the 1990s.

- Appeared in the 2005 movie *The Longest Yard with Adam Sandler*, as a basketball player who later becomes a wide receiver for the Mean Machine football team.

- Even though Michael Irvin is originally from Miami, Florida, he was inducted into the Texas Sports Hall of Fame in 2008, the same year he made it into the Pro Football Hall of Fame.

- He is an outspoken Christian, and has said that his faith has helped him through the darkest times of his life.

- He's nicknamed "Playmaker" for his ability to make big-time, clutch plays in his college career at Miami, and his pro career with the Cowboys.

- He set University of Miami records for most receptions (143) and touchdown catches (26) in a career.

- Helped Miami win the 1987 National Championship over top-ranked Oklahoma.

- Was coached by Jimmy Johnson both in college at Miami and in the NFL with Dallas.

1. How many Super Bowl rings does Michael Irvin have?

2. True or False: Michael Irvin has more than 700 career catches with the Cowboys.

3. How many career touchdown catches does Michael Irvin have?

4. True or False: Michael Irvin has less than 10,000 receiving yards.

5. Where does Michael Irvin rank on the NFL's all-time receiving yards list?

6. How many times did Michael Irvin lead the NFL in receiving yards in a season?

7. What famous reality show did Michael Irvin compete in?

8. By the time he retired in 1999, Michael Irvin set how many receiving records?

9. Michael Irvin is a playmaker. How many 100-yard receiving games did he have in his career?

10. True or False: Michael Irvin was an easygoing, laid back player who didn't talk much.

ANSWER

1. He's won three Super Bowls with the Dallas Cowboys, in 1992, 1993 and 1995.
2. True! Over the course of his career, Michael Irvin has racked up 750 catches for Dallas.
3. 65.
4. False. He's got 11,904 receiving yards in his career.
5. He's #30 overall.
6. Surprisingly, he only led the league in receiving yards once, in 1991. He had 1,523 receiving yards that season.
7. He competed in Dancing with the Stars.
8. 20 different Cowboys receiving records.
9. 47.
10. False! He was extremely talkative, and would routinely talk smack all game long with opposing defensive backs! But the most important thing? He often backed it up!

"You tell everyone or anyone that has ever doubted, thought they didn't measure up or wanted to quit - look up get up and don't ever give up."

"Through the times I've gone through the last couple of weeks - and I'm still trying to help a friend - I got attacked pretty hard through the media, and it hurt and it was devastating, but I really found out who was with me and who was there for me."

"The movie, 'Remember the Titans,' is my favorite movie, staring Denzel Washington. I love the way in this movie the game of football brings those boys together, it unites those boys on that football field. It unites a whole town, black, white, old, young, rich and poor."

"I didn't always know, but I always wanted to. I always wanted to be the very best receiver the Cowboys ever had. That was my goal coming in as a rookie and my goal throughout my career: being the best they ever had, going up in the Ring of Honor."

"Most train to be part of the game. The greatest train to be the game: I am the game. Third-and-9, two-minutes left, that's what I train for. I train for moments everyone runs from. I run for them."

LESSONS FROM THE STORY

- Take care of family, even when hard times hit.

- When parents and family support your passion, it helps you to be all that you can be.

- Honor your parents.

- Help them out any way you can around the house.

- Reflect on the good qualities your parents have taught you or given you.

15

JOSH JACOBS

FROM RAGS TO RICHES

If you think about it, every NFL player has had to overcome their own share of obstacles in order to play the game we all love. Even the first-round picks who are expected to be superstars have had to overcome something so they could make it to the big time. And perhaps nobody is a bigger example of this than Raiders starting running back Josh Jacobs.

We all see what he does on the football field when the lights are shining on him, and he's on primetime TV. He's one of the league's superstars. But the vast majority of people did not see what he had to go through in order to get where he is today. He might be a multimillionaire living in Las Vegas right now. But there was one point where he was homeless. Along with his dad and four siblings.

Even though Marty Jacobs was awarded custody of young Josh and his brother and two sisters, he struggled to make ends meet and all five of them often had to live out of his car. If they ever did scrounge up enough money to find a place to stay, they were only able to stay in various hotel rooms one night at a time before they had to pack up, and continue life on the road.

But after all the struggles, sleepless nights, and empty bellies, Josh found something that would eventually help him rise above his circumstances: the game of football itself. Josh may have been dirt poor at this point in his life, but he was richly blessed with athletic talent. And when he played football for the McLain High School Titans near where he grew up in Tulsa, Oklahoma, that would be his way of showing the world just how much talent he possessed. But it wouldn't be easy to get everyone's attention.

During his high school career, Jacobs rushed for over 5,300 yards and 56 touchdowns. But even after a spectacular four years, he didn't get his first scholarship offer until late in his senior season. That's when one of his high school coaches who was also a recruiting coordinator, stepped in. While most players who aspire to play college football would get scouted or send in highlights of their skills to colleges on DVD or online, Coach Gerald Smith suggested that Josh use a different platform to get people to notice him—Twitter.

So Josh began posting his high school highlights on Twitter. And it wasn't long before bigger schools came knocking at his door. This included his home state college team, the Oklahoma Sooners, Oklahoma State, Purdue, Iowa State, Northern Iowa, Missouri, TCU, Texas, and others. But the one school that stood out to Jacobs was Alabama, coached by the legendary Nick Saban. But Jacobs was a three-star recruit when he committed to play football for the Crimson Tide. Being a three-star recruit at Alabama is like trying to make an NFL team as a sixth- or seventh-round draft pick. It doesn't usually happen. Alabama only takes the best of the best.

But Josh Jacobs gritted his teeth, began his uphill climb, and continued to do what he did best: outwork everyone else on the team. In fact, he worked so hard that he earned some playing time as a true freshman in 2016. He worked hard enough to impress Coach Saban, which is almost impossible to do. As a freshman in 2016, Jacobs carried the ball 86 times for 564 yards and 4 touchdowns. But it's what he would do later on in his college career that would show how hard he was willing to work to make his NFL dream a reality.

After his second season with the Tide in 2017, it was revealed that Josh had been playing on a broken ankle for most of the year. The next year, he continued to show his toughness. He was named the MVP of the 2018 SEC Championship Game in Alabama's 35-28 win over Georgia. Not only did he rush for 83 yards and a pair of touchdowns, but he was also doing it all while suffering from the flu. He had to be given IVs before, during and after the game. He also had a tough time breathing. He said he "felt like he was dying" every time he came off the field. But his work ethic would not let him quit.

He did whatever it took to help his team win. Whether it was playing football while he had a broken ankle, the flu, or by playing on special teams, Josh didn't care as long as he did his best, and it helped Alabama win. This toughness and stubborn refusal to give up caught the eye of the Las Vegas Raiders, who took Josh in the first round with the 24th overall pick.

He was now a professional football player. The homeless kid, who didn't have much to eat, and little to no money, was now a player for the Oakland Raiders. And he was due to make BIG money on his rookie contract. More money than most people ever see in their entire lives! When he officially signed with the Raiders, Jacobs earned a $6.7 million signing bonus as part of a contract that was worth up to almost $12 million. And instead of blowing his money on fancy clothes, expensive jewelry, or anything else like that, Jacobs' first purchase with his newfound wealth was to buy his dad a house. He never forgot where he came from.

He's now one of the best running backs in the entire NFL. But at his core, Josh Jacobs is still a kid from Tulsa, Oklahoma who continues to grind, scratch, claw and fight for every bit of success that he has gotten. On the field for the Silver and Black, Jacobs embodies this tough mentality by being a strong, physical running back. He certainly can make moves when he has to. But his defining characteristic as a running back, is to run through or over defenders rather than around them. Las Vegas may be a flashy city where people go to party. But the Raiders have found their franchise player of the future, and he's blue collar to the core.

In an interview with ESPN shortly after buying his dad the house, Josh Jacobs simply said that growing up in extreme poverty taught him to be appreciative of all that he did have. Even if it wasn't much at the time. "It definitely helped mold me because I learned to respect the little things. And just to appreciate the things that I have, being with my family, and those who care about me a lot."

Josh learned a lot from his dad Marty on what it meant to be a real man. And now that Josh is a father himself with a young son, Marty Jacobs is proud of what his boy has done. "He's a good dad. He's trying to do everything he can to provide, and make sure that he's never put in that situation again. That's all I hope for. I want success for all my children at whatever level. They don't have to be Josh-level. They can be wherever they're at in their life. Just to be the best parents they can be, and just carry on and go forward in life."

The story of Josh Jacobs so far has been an amazing one. But at the core, it's a story that is remarkably relatable to a lot of people. A son learns a lot from his parent through tough times. He figures out a way he can help himself, his father, and his siblings escape a rough situation. And then when he does escape the bad situation, the first thing he does is to thank his father by giving back. And the cycle of good parenting continues with children of his own.

That is the story of Josh Jacobs, and many, many other people in a nutshell. What do they all have in common? They all are grateful, and humble. They could be bitter, angry, and sad about their life situation. But they're not; they just choose to put their head down, work hard, and fight their way out of it until they get to where they want to be.

If you or your family is struggling to get to a better situation in your own life, be like Josh Jacobs. Work hard and continue to fight to escape your situation in the best way that you know how. But above all, remain grateful for the positives in every day. Even if they may be hard to see at times and if you make it out of the bad situation, stay humble and never forget where you came from!

BONUS

Unlock an exclusive treasure trove of football knowledge with our bonus content: 100 Unique Football Facts and Trivia Questions. This special collection will enrich your understanding of the game and provide you with captivating trivia to impress friends and family. From iconic moments in football history to intriguing facts about legendary players, this content is perfect for deepening your appreciation of the sport. Enhance your journey with these fascinating insights and become a true football aficionado. Whether you're a lifelong fan or new to the game, this bonus content will provide hours of enjoyment. Get ready to explore the wonders of football like never before.

To access your bonus content, simply scan the QR code below with your smartphone and dive into the world of football!

- Was born on February 11, 1998 in Tulsa, Oklahoma.

- Was kicked out of the house by his mother when he was growing up, when he sided with his dad.

- Living in a rough part of Tulsa toughened him up as a kid before he finally made it out.

- Played college football for Alabama from 2016-2018.

- Drafted by the Raiders in the first round of the 2019 NFL Draft, with the 24th overall pick.

- His younger brother Isaiah Jacobs is a running back for the UAB Blazers college football team based in Birmingham, Alabama.

- Is part Filipino from his paternal grandmother.

- Was part of a Kia commercial that aired during the Super Bowl. The commercial showed what his experience was like growing up.

- He's both a tough running back, and can be a versatile receiver when he has to be. He's a powerful runner and an elusive wide receiver!

- He's a shy, quiet guy. But he lets his running and play on the field talk for him!

1. True or False: Josh Jacobs often had to move from hotel to hotel growing up when he was living with his father.

2. True or False: Josh Jacobs rushed for over 5,000 yards in high school.

3. Which teams has Josh Jacobs played for in his career?

4. How many times has Josh Jacobs been to the Pro Bowl?

5. True or False: Josh Jacobs led the NFL in rushing yards in 2022.

6. What number does Josh Jacobs currently wear for the Packers?

7. True or False: His yards per carry average is over four yards per carry.

8. What faith is Josh Jacobs?

9. True or False: Josh Jacobs played with a broken ankle for most of his sophomore season at Alabama.

10. True or False: Josh Jacobs has a son named Braxton.

ANSWER

1. True.
2. True! He ran for 5,372 yards when he played for McClain High School.
3. He has played for the Las Vegas Raiders, and just recently signed as a
4. free agent to play for the Green Bay Packers in the 2024 season.
   He's a two-time Pro Bowler.
5. True! He had a staggering 1,653 yards for the Raiders in 2022!
6. #8
   True! His current average so far is 4.2 yards per carry, which means he's
7. a solid, consistent running back!
8. Josh Jacobs is a Christian.
9. True!
10. True!

"It's crazy how it all played out. I didn't know what it took or how much was needed to get here. I just did the best that I could. That's what all the teams told me. I guess the production I put on tape was huge."

"The thing about it is that you have to remain who you are. I still see myself the same way I did four years ago. I still don't think I'm better than people. I still look at myself as a regular person. When you view it that way, it keeps you level-headed. You don't really notice all of this."

"My father would give her a stack of money. She would go out and spend it and we'd be eating Salvation Army food. I would ask her how she could go spend that money and not have good food for us to eat. She didn't like that, how I rebelled and spoke up. So she kicked me out."

"I wanted to play on the biggest stage I could find. When you've been underrated your whole life, you have a point to prove."

"I never was one of those people who had the dream of going to NFL," I was just happy because I was the first person to ever go to college in my family. Once I got to the college level, I just wanted to compete at a high level. And once I blew up like I did, I was like, 'Wow.' Now I get to be on the biggest stage ever. It's crazy to think about everything that's happening. And It's definitely humbling to think about how I got here."

LESSONS FROM THE STORY

- Everyone who is now great at what they do had to start somewhere.

- Even if you aren't noticed right away for being good at what you do, keep practicing and keep pushing.

- If you're not as talented as someone else, there's only one guaranteed way to beat them: Outwork them.

- Think of others before yourself.

- Never forget where you came from.

16

2009 NEW ORLEANS SAINTS

WINNING AFTER TRAGEDY

Sports always have the potential to bring people together. Whether it's your middle school or high school team, or favorite college team, fans live through their favorite players on the field. In the case of the Saints, the city of New Orleans took supporting their favorite team to the next level. But their love for the Saints went far beyond just rooting for their hometown team. Especially in 2009, four short years after a true tragedy.

In late August, one of the strongest hurricanes on record, Hurricane Katrina, slammed into New Orleans, and flooded around 80% of the city. In some ways, the Big Easy is still recovering from the disaster. But the 2009 New Orleans Saints gave the city the one thing it needed the most at that time—hope.

Like the 1980 United States Hockey Team that beat the Soviets in the Miracle on Ice, "Cinderella Man" Jim Braddock winning the Heavyweight Championship of the World in boxing, and Vince Papale making the Philadelphia Eagles in an "Invincible" comeback, the New Orleans Saints gave their city hope for the future. Even when the city was still rebuilding from Hurricane Katrina, all 390,000 people rallied around them.

The Saints fed off the city's support. They ripped off 13 straight wins for a 13-0 start before they lost their first game. This was a franchise record at the time. Hall of Fame quarterback Drew Brees was also having one of the best years of his career. He threw for almost 4,400 yards and 34 touchdowns. On defense, New Orleans was led by hard-hitting linebacker Jonathan Vilma, and safeties Darren Sharper and Roman Harper. Behind Brees' efficient and explosive season under center, and a stout defense, New Orleans rolled to a surprising 13-3 record!

This was more than the city could have hoped for. Only four years after New Orleans was destroyed by one of the most devastating storms in history, the Saints gave the city hope. While football is only a game, the team just helped New Orleans escape reality. Things were tough at the time, and they would be for many years after. But for at least one season, Coach Sean Payton and his team helped the people in the Big Easy forget about having to pick up the pieces and rebuild everything. Even if it was just for a little while.

But there was nothing forgettable about the run the Saints were on. They rolled into the postseason as the top team in the NFC, the first time they had ever done that. There was magic surrounding the team. Especially when they played in their first playoff game against Arizona Cardinals, led by another Hall of Famer in Kurt Warner.

Even though it had been 10 years since he led the Rams to a Super Bowl Championship, Warner was still a dangerous quarterback at 38 years old. Along with that, he had Larry Fitzgerald, a future Hall of Fame wide receiver in his prime. But none of that mattered. The Saints were on another level in that game, blowing out the Cardinals by a final score of 45-14 to advance to the NFC Championship Game for the first time ever!

New Orleans' dream season would soon be seriously tested though, when they played the Minnesota Vikings, and veteran gunslinger and Hall of Famer Brett Favre. Brett Favre and Drew Brees were in opposite stages of their careers in 2009. Brees was playing the best football of his life, and in his prime at 30 years old. Brett Favre on the other hand, was looking for his second Super Bowl Championship, and was pushing 40 years old. He was past his glory days with Green Bay, but he still represented Minnesota's best shot of getting back to the Super Bowl for the first time since 1976.

The 2009 NFC Championship was only the third time that overtime was needed to decide who would advance to the Super Bowl. It was a back and forth, tense, nerve-wracking game. This contest had everything! From explosive plays, tons of turnovers by both teams, right down to a game-deciding field goal, everyone was on the edge of their seats right up until the final seconds. Drew Brees only went 17-31 passing for 197 yards, but he threw three touchdown passes when the team needed him the most. Brett Favre exploded that day, throwing for 310 yards and a touchdown.

However, the Saints' last and best chance of advancing to Super Bowl 44 in Miami, Florida, would come down to the right leg of 22-year-old kicker Garrett Hartley. But surprisingly, Hartley called his dad the morning of the NFC Championship Game around 2am and told him the dream that he'd had. In an interview with WDSU Channel 6, Hartley dreamed he would kick a 42-yard field goal from the right hashmark to send the Saints to the Super Bowl. "I was like, 'Dad, I just have a weird feeling it's going to be a 42-yarder on the right hash. It's going to come down to it," he said.

A few hours after the fateful dream and phone call with his dad, Hartley's dream came true. He booted the field goal straight through the uprights, hugged backup quarterback Mark Brunell, and simply told him, "We're going to Miami!"

The Saints had defeated the Vikings 31-28, and punched their ticket to Super Bowl 44 to face Peyton Manning and the Indianapolis Colts. But like Brett Favre, Manning would be another huge obstacle. The last one. The Colts would be the final thing standing in between the Saints and a World Championship. But it wouldn't be easy. Manning was having an MVP season. He threw for over 4,500 yards and 33 touchdowns, and the Colts won their first 14 games of the season before finishing 14-2. Indy was clicking, and they wouldn't let an upstart Saints team ruin their dream!

The Colts raced out to an early 10-0 lead, and looked dominant on defense. They sacked Drew Brees and kept the Saints offense from taking off, as they led a tight game at halftime, 10-6. But Saints coach Sean Payton had an ace up his sleeve that caught the Colts by surprise: an onside kick! That showed he was willing to do whatever it took to win for the city of New Orleans. Even though it was the Saints' first appearance in the big game, they weren't just happy to be here; they were here to WIN!

And the team battled like that for the rest of the night, until they were up 24-17 with under four minutes left in the game. But they were facing a four-time MVP in Peyton Manning. He knew what it took to win a Super Bowl ring. He had beaten the Bears in Super Bowl 41 three years earlier.

The Saints defense would have to buckle down, man up, and finish off the biggest game of their lives. They'd have to find a way to beat the NFL MVP on the world's biggest stage with millions of people watching. Especially their fans. This one would be for everyone affected by Hurricane Katrina. The hope and support of a battered but strong city, had pushed this team to heights nobody believed were possible. But there was one final step left to take before they were on top of the world.

Peyton Manning was the NFL MVP that year. But for as great as he is, even he makes mistakes. And a rare mistake from him would seal the game for the Saints. With the Colts marching down the field to tie the game and threatening to score, Saints cornerback Tracy Porter jumped in front of a pass by Peyton Manning, and ran it back 74 yards for a touchdown! The Port Allen, Louisiana kid just sealed a win in the Super Bowl for his home team. Saints win, 31-17!

The underdogs from the Big Easy had done the impossible. The improbable dream had come true. They were bringing the Lombardi Trophy back to a city and region that needed it more than anyone else in the absolute worst way. This victory showed that anything can be overcome, from an MVP quarterback, to a Category 5 hurricane, to picking up the pieces after. But the road back always begins with hope.

Whatever you're going through in your life, have hope in the future, and have faith in yourself and those around you. If you fight through every obstacle you have in your life, and surround yourself with the right friends and family, you have the power to reach your dreams. Just like Drew Brees, Sean Payton, and the 2009 New Orleans Saints!

- Started the 2009 season with an 8-0 record, which was the best mark in team history.

- The team eventually set the record for wins in franchise history.

- They had finished last in the NFC South the year before with an 8-8 record. They went from worst to first in their division!

- Went on to start the season 13-0 before losing their first game

- The Saints scored nearly 32 points per game, which led the league.

- The defense was also forcing at least two turnovers a game.

- They had a balanced rushing attack, which had three running backs, Pierre Thomas, Mike Bell and Reggie Bush, all gain over 300 yards that season.

- The 2009 Saints became the first team in NFL history to defeat three Super Bowl-winning quarterbacks on the way to winning their first title (Kurt Warner, Brett Favre, Peyton Manning).

- After Hurricane Katrina, the New Orleans Superdome was used as a shelter for displaced people.

- Despite having the best record they'd ever had, the Saints were underdogs in Super Bowl 44.

1. Who coached the Saints during the 2009 season?

2. What is the stadium called where the Saints play their home games?

3. How many Pro Bowlers did the Saints have on their 2009 team?

4. True or False: Every one of the Pro Bowlers participated in the 2010 Pro Bowl.

5. How many wins did the Saints get in the regular season?

6. True or False: Even with 13 wins, the Saints didn't have the best record in the NFL.

7. Who had the best record in the NFL during the 2009 season? Hint: It's who the Saints played in the Super Bowl.

8. Which Hall of Fame quarterback did the Saints beat to get to the Super Bowl in 2009?

9. How much were the Colts favored to win Super Bowl 44?

10. What ended up being the final score of Super Bowl 44?

ANSWER

1. *Sean Payton.*
2. *The Louisiana Superdome*
3. *Seven Pro Bowlers, led by Hall of Fame Quarterback Drew Brees!*
4. *False. None of them did. They sat out to avoid getting injured since the Pro Bowl had been traditionally held the week before the Super Bowl.*
5. *They racked up 13 wins.*
6. *True. They were tied with the Chargers for the second-best record in the league.*
7. *The Indianapolis Colts went 14-2 that season.*
8. *Brett Favre.*
9. *They were favored to beat New Orleans by five points, a solid margin.*
10. *The Saints ended up surprising and upsetting the Colts by beating them by two touchdowns, 31-17!*

"A lot of fans would explain to us that this was their break from their reality," said former Saints linebacker Jonathan Vilma. "So they wanted to go and get there early, tailgate, get away from whatever problems that they had going on." -Saints LB Jonathan Vilma

"He knew how to keep perspective on the season, how to keep perspective on the offense, how to keep perspective on the team." -Jonathan Vilma talking about quarterback Drew Brees

"When you get locked into the grind of the NFL season, you kind of forget what's going on in the outside world," Vilma said. "To take a Tuesday, four or five hours out of the day, it was really humbling to regain perspective on what's going on around you in the community." Jonathan Vilma.

"I'll never forget, and I know my teammates will never forget, when we won the NFC Championship Game and, for that night, there was no crime in the city -- first time ever," said Vilma.
"That's when we knew they live and die with the Saints, how we play. Win, lose or draw they always appreciated if we gave 110 percent." -Jonathan Vilma

"I don't remember talking to anybody. You look up and see the confetti dropping -- everyone's jumping around, cheering. I don't know if I ever said a word besides, 'I can't believe this.' That was the only thing I kept saying." -Jonathan Vilma

FIVE LESSONS FROM THE STORY

- Sometimes a community needs something to give it hope.

- Have trust in your family, friends and teammates.

- Have confidence in yourself to rise to the occasion when the time comes.

- Enjoy the journey, instead of worrying about the destination.

- Sports have the potential to bring entire communities together.

17

JOE THOMAS

MR. CONSISTENCY

Offensive linemen are the unsung heroes of football. Without the big guys up front, it doesn't matter how talented your team is, you're not going anywhere. You won't be able to move the ball down the field, and your quarterback will always be sore the morning after the game if his linemen don't keep him safe.

While the center is the anchor of any offensive line, the left tackle is the lineman most responsible for protecting the quarterback. Most quarterbacks are right-handed, which means their back is turned toward the left side of the field when they throw. They're not able to see that side of the field and are easily sacked if there isn't a great left tackle there to protect them. But this story is about one of the greatest left tackles NFL history: Joe Thomas of the Cleveland Browns!

Thomas wasn't just one of the most consistent left tackles of all time, he was one of the most consistent players of all time, no matter what was going on around him. Whether he was on a truly bad Browns football team, he was playing through pain, or if he was protecting one of 20 different quarterbacks over his career, he was always blocking and playing at a ridiculously high level.

There were many seasons where the Browns were an awful football team. In fact, the Browns' overall record during Thomas's 11 seasons in the NFL was a miserable 48-119. The team only won an average of four games a year with Thomas on the offensive line. Any normal player in that situation would be dying to be traded to a winning team. Could anybody blame them?

But Joe Thomas stuck it out his entire career. He was loyal to the team that drafted him in 2007. He developed a bond with the city of Cleveland and its fans that he refused to let go of, and he was as blue collar as they come. In fact, when he was drafted, Thomas wasn't in New York City wearing a flashy suit and rubbing elbows with celebrities on Draft night like the other future stars of the NFL. Instead, he was out on the waters of Lake Michigan fishing with his dad and buddies when he got a phone call that the Browns had selected him with the third overall pick. That showed his humility. He was humble, and ready to get to work whenever his name was called.

Along with being humble and hardworking, Joe Thomas was also obsessed with attention to detail. Linemen are not considered "skill players" like quarterbacks, running backs and wide receivers. But I've always found that ironic. Especially because Thomas learned every skill that he possibly needed to know to be successful as a left tackle. He was relentless in studying film, figuring out his opponents' tendencies, and learning what the best moves were to gain leverage so he could move the guy across from him out of the play, and keep his quarterback safe. His obsession with the small things went all the way down to the tiniest detail.

In an interview with NFL.com, Thomas's teammate and former Browns kicker Phil Dawson marveled at how well the big left tackle prepared himself before games: "He always was ready, he studied his opponents, he knew all their tendencies, he knew all their tells. He'd know what was coming before they did. And when you combine knowing what your opponent's going to do and your attention to detail with your technique, coupled with elite athletic ability, I mean, that's why you're Joe Thomas."

And not only was Thomas consistently prepared the best he could be, he also never took a play off. I mean that literally. The guy played 10,363 straight snaps. From his first play as a rookie in 2007, to his final play in a game in late October 2017, Joe Thomas never took a play off. He never slacked off on anything. For any reason.

He could be struggling with pain, he could be frustrated after all the Browns' numerous losses, or adjusting to learning how to protect a new quarterback. But he never quit on his team. Ever. The only thing that eventually took him out of the game was a knee injury that forced him to retire at 33 years old. But he never slacked off, never complained, and never acted like a diva. He was the anchor on the Browns' offensive line.

This level of consistency was noticed by everyone who knew him, or saw him play. And it was noticed and rewarded by the NFL, too. Despite the Browns being an awful team for most of his career, Joe Thomas earned 10 consecutive Pro Bowl selections from 2007 to 2016, and was a six-time first team All-Pro. There are few players in league history, if any, who have been as consistent as him.

If you ask Joe Thomas what he's most proud of, I'm sure he'd smile at the awards he's earned over his career. In an interview shortly after being named a Hall of Famer, Thomas said staying consistent is what he was most proud of during his time as a Cleveland Brown:

"The one theme that has been, probably, the thing I hold most closely to my heart when people ask about 'What are you most proud of during your career,' it's that snap streak because of what it represents to me," Thomas said. "'Count on me.' That was always the motto I had in my head. It was 'Count on me.' When times get tough, and you want to know who to look at, count on me. You know you can slide to my side. 'Count on me' was something that was ingrained in my brain, ingrained in my character from when I was a little boy. It's always just been part of my identity, and I think that's why that snap streak is the most special thing I think about when I think about my career."

Along with being reliable on the field, the big left tackle had an even bigger heart when he wasn't playing. He loved his teammates and friends and being a Cleveland Brown so much that when the Denver Broncos attempted to get Joe Thomas in a trade near the end of his career, the possibility of leaving Cleveland behind broke his heart.

His teammates were happy for him and wanted him to go chase a Super Bowl with a great team. Denver did end up winning it all that year, but Joe Thomas valued his legacy, and what he had built over the years, more than he valued chasing rings. Because of his hard work, loyalty, and incredible consistency, Joe Thomas was eventually inducted into the Pro Football Hall of Fame on August 5, 2023.

Joe Thomas's career can serve as an inspiration for you. You might have big goals and dreams. Fantastic! Go for it! But how do you get there? You don't get there overnight. You achieve your dreams like Joe Thomas achieved his: by doing the little things right.

Instead of playing videogames, maybe study a little bit more, and write more detailed notes for that test. Instead of giving up when things get hard, stick it out and keep going. If you're having a bad day, don't wallow in sadness. Get up, dust yourself off, and keep going. Joe didn't take a play or game off. If you want to be Joe Thomas–level great at anything you're doing, you can't take time off either.

If your friends and family matter to you, show them they matter by showing up for them every day. Help your parents around the house with chores and listen to them as they try to give you their wisdom. Joe Thomas became one of the greatest players in NFL history partly because he listened to his parents, Eric and Sally Thomas, and took what they taught him to heart.

Be there for your friends and family in their best and worst times. Joe Thomas was there for his friends and teammates in Cleveland, even when times were the absolute worst. He never ran away. He was loyal to them. Loyalty doesn't cost anything other than to truly care about someone other than yourself.

Lastly, remain humble in all that you do. When someone is the greatest at something, whether it's a hobby, their job or a certain skill, it's easy to get cocky and overconfident. But true champions stay humble, quiet, and let their hard work do the talking for them. That's how Joe Thomas approached his career with the Browns, and that's how you can approach life as you grow up and fulfill your purpose. If you do all these things then greatness will come!

- Born on December 4th, 1984 in Brookfield, Wisconsin.

- His height and weight during his playing days was 6'6 and 312 pounds! He's massive!

- Played left tackle.

- Played for the Wisconsin Badgers college football team from 2003-2006.

- Drafted by the Cleveland Browns with the third overall pick in the 2007 NFL Draft.

- Played for the Browns for 11 seasons, from 2007-2017.

- Made the Pro Bowl 10 times!

- He was named to the NFL's All-Decade Team of the 2010s.

- He is in both the College Football and Pro Football Halls of Fame.

- Widely considered to be one of, if not the, greatest left tackles in NFL history.

1. True or False: Joe Thomas was in New York City the night he was drafted by the Browns.

2. How many consecutive snaps did Joe Thomas play for the Browns?

3. True or False: Joe Thomas unfortunately never made the Playoffs while he was a member of the Browns.

4. True or False: The Denver Broncos wanted to trade for Joe Thomas.

5. Joe Thomas currently coaches for which team?

6. True or False: Joe Thomas lost 50 pounds after he retired in 2017.

7. True or False: Joe Thomas is the first Cleveland Browns player to make it to the Pro Football Hall of Fame since the team was reactivated in 1999.

8. True or False: Joe Thomas and his wife were both athletes in college.

9. How many children does Joe Thomas have?

10. When was Joe Thomas inducted into the Pro Football Hall of Fame?

ANSWER

1. False! Joe was fishing on Lake Michigan with his father and buddies when the Browns drafted him.
2. 10,363 consecutive snaps!
3. True. Even though Cleveland won 10 games in his rookie year, Joe Thomas sadly never got to play in a playoff game for the Browns.
4. True! The Broncos were trying to make a Super Bowl run, while the Browns were having an awful season. But Joe Thomas turned them down.
5. He currently is the offensive line coach for the Munich Ravens of the European League of Football.
6. True! He's still huge, but he's around 260 pounds instead of over 310 pounds.
7. True! The Browns have several other Hall of Famers enshrined in Canton, Ohio. But it's been a long time since they've added one. Joe Thomas was the first new one!
8. True. Joe and Annie Thomas were both athletes. He played football, while she was a star player on the Wisconsin women's basketball team.
9. Joe Thomas has four children.
10. 2023.

QUOTES

"My mentality from the day I started playing sports was that you get up, you dust yourself off and you do it again."

"Coming in, you're so concerned about learning your job and the things you need to do to be successful individually. Once that's good, you can start to focus on learning guys around you and learning defenses and what they're trying to do to you."

"Count on me. That was my motto."

"I'm a Clevelander. I've spent the majority of my adult life here. Every day when I come to work, it's 'Let's turn this team into a consistent winner.' Because it would be such a special story."

"The passion, toughness and determination that you display on a daily basis is an inspiration for myself and for all of my teammates and all the people that wear 'Cleveland' across their chest."

LESSONS FROM THE STORY

- Do the little things right. And do them over and over again.

- Be dependable and reliable for your friends and family in whatever you are doing.

- Being loyal pays off.

- Before a big test or anything else, study as much as you can. Prepare well.

- If you are successful and reach your dreams, thank your parents. They'll appreciate it.

18

1993 AFC WILD CARD GAME

GREATEST COMEBACK IN NFL HISTORY

If you've ever played a sport, and someone was hurt, or your team was down at a key point in the game, I'm sure you've heard these three words from your coaches: next man up. For some people, it's just a cliché saying. But for the 1992 Buffalo Bills, they took that mentality to heart.

Following a bad loss to the Houston Oilers to end the regular season, Buffalo was not only set to face Houston the very next week in the Playoffs, but they were also going to be forced to play them without their All-Pro quarterback Jim Kelly, who had strained ligaments in his knee.

Even worse for the Bills, the man replacing Kelly for the Wild Card Game was Frank Reich, who had an awful game to end the season, when he went just 11-23 for 99 yards and 2 interceptions. But the Bills still felt confident going into the Playoffs against the Oilers, because they'd be playing in front of a packed house at home in Orchard Park, New York.

Hall of Fame wide receiver Andre Reed remembers feeling good going into the game: "We had them at home. We felt good being home," Reed said. "We were pretty good at home all year. We were going to use the crowd to our advantage."

Unfortunately for Reed and the Bills, on January 3, 1993, everything that could go wrong went wrong. The Oilers picked up right where they left off, as they rolled to a 28-3 halftime lead. Houston's quarterback, Warren Moon had arguably his best half as a pro, when he went 19-22 for 218 yards and 4 touchdowns.

In the Buffalo locker room at halftime, the Bills were predictably downtrodden. They had a defeated mindset. Their defensive coordinator Walt Corey lit them up, ripping them a new one to fire them up for the second half. Years after the game, Corey said, "I can't repeat the words, but the more I talked, the louder I got. To me, they looked timid. This is an attitude game. Sometimes you start playing, and you're afraid to make things happen, or you're afraid to make a mistake."

Head coach Marv Levy also tuned his team up, saying, "You've got thirty more minutes. Maybe it's the last thirty minutes of your season. When your season's over, you're going to have to live with yourselves and look yourselves in the eyes. You'd better have a reason to feel good about yourselves, regardless of how this game turns out."

Levy and Corey both appealed to the Bills' sense of pride in themselves and their teammates. After all, the team had been to the Super Bowl the previous year. They were the defending AFC Champions. They knew what it took to compete for pro football's ultimate prize.

But to get back to the big game, they had to climb football's version of Mount Everest. It was looming in front of them, and it only got bigger. Not only did Houston's Bubba McDowell intercept Frank Reich early in the second half, and return the pass all the way for a touchdown, the Bills also lost their starting running back Thurman Thomas to a hip injury.

So now, not only were the Bills down by a staggering 32 points, but they were also going to have to mount a comeback with their second-string quarterback and running back. Their backs were really up against the wall now. It was a do or die situation.

But for as bad as the Bills had played, and for as poor as their luck was all day long, things began to change. Mother Nature must've been a Bills fan that day, because on the ensuing kickoff, the wind shifted the ball just before it was kicked by Houston's Al Del Greco. Buffalo linebacker Mark Maddox recovered the ball at the 50-yard line, and from that point on, the Bills would score a touchdown not just on that drive, but on four straight second half drives to cut Houston's lead to 35-31. And the Bills did all this in a span of just 6:52 of game time.

As for the third quarter, the Bills had outscored Houston 28-7, and held the Oilers' talented quarterback, Warren Moon, to just 2-7 passing for only 19 yards. What was once a sure win, seemed to be slowly slipping out of Houston's fingers.

But even though the Oilers' Top 10 defense had given up nearly 30 points, they were still too good to go away quietly. Houston forced the Bills to punt, and the Oilers' offense began to march down the field like they had done all day long. Warren Moon connected with his receivers on what seemed like pass after pass, until Houston found themselves at Buffalo's 14-yard line, and leading the game 35-31. They were still threatening to spoil the rally, and send the defending AFC Champs home for the rest of the winter.

Oilers kicker Al Del Greco was all set to attempt a chip shot field goal from 31 yards away. A made field goal would get Houston closer to a matchup with Pittsburgh in the Divisional Game the following week. But he never got the chance to even try the field goal. After the snap was botched, Buffalo recovered the football at their own 26-yard line, and they began what would be the go-ahead drive if they could score a touchdown.

Frank Reich might have been a backup quarterback. But he looked like a seasoned field general as he led Buffalo down the field. He drove the Bills 74 yards in just five plays, and threw a touchdown pass to Andre Reed. What once seemed like an insurmountable deficit, was now completely erased. The Bills led 38-35, with just 3:08 remaining in the game.

Unfortunately for the Bills, their defense couldn't contain the elusive Warren Moon, and he led the Oilers down the field on a 63-yard drive that ended with a tying field goal. The madness of overtime was here. All the chips were pushed into the center of the table. The winner advanced. The loser's season would be over.

Houston got the ball first on their own 20-yard line. But on the third pass of the drive, Warren Moon was intercepted by Buffalo's Nate Odomes. Odomes' interception, coupled with a facemask on the Oilers, gave the Bills a first down at Houston's 20-yard line.

The moment was now here. Buffalo had fought all the way back. They had overcome a mountain of mistakes, injuries and great plays by Houston. And they were right there, ready to send out veteran kicker Steve Christie. Foot met ball a few seconds later, and Steve Christie was absolutely clutch. He drilled the game winning field goal without even thinking about it to give the Bills a 41-38 win, and he drove a dagger through the hearts of Houston fans everywhere.

While Bills players were ecstatic, it was the exact opposite in the Houston locker room after the game. Oilers cornerback Cris Dishman was blunt: "We definitely choked. We got outcoached, outplayed. There's no way we blow a 32-point lead with the talent we have. They made adjustments good enough to win the game. We didn't."

But while Houston let the win slip from their fingers, Buffalo proved two important points: Any team can win on any given Sunday, and that games are never truly over until the final whistle blows. In the same way, nothing you pursue in life is never truly out of your grasp. That is, unless you willingly let it go. Giving up is a conscious choice. But so is choosing to continue fighting, even when the odds may be firmly stacked against you.

The Bills not only won that game against the Oilers, they also made a return trip to the Super Bowl that year. How? They never lost faith in themselves, each other, or their coaching staff. Even when they were down by five scores. Never lose faith in yourself or those around you, whether it's in sports or in life. You never know what might happen. A little bit of belief can always spark a BIG comeback!

- Stood as the greatest comeback in NFL history for almost 30 years until the Minnesota Vikings came back to beat the Colts in 2022 after being down 33 points.

- Even though the game was in Buffalo, it was blacked out. A lot of Bills fans weren't able to watch the game on TV.

- Frank Reich, the man who quarterbacked Buffalo to the second-largest comeback victory in NFL history, was also the coach to be on the losing side of the biggest comeback in history. His Colts eventually fell to the Vikings 39-36 after being up by 33 points at halftime.

- The Bills overcame a 35-3 deficit to beat the Oilers.

- The game was listed as #1 on the list of the NFL's Top 10 Comebacks.

- Most of the fans began to leave the stadium when the Bills were down by multiple scores.

- While the game in Buffalo is known as The Comeback, it's always known as The Choke in Houston.

- The Bills outscored the Oilers 38-10 in the second half and overtime to win the game.

- Warren Moon, the Hall of Fame quarterback, was on the losing side of the game for the Oilers.

- Frank Reich threw for 289 yards and four touchdowns that day, as he led the Bills to the improbable victory.

1. Who did Frank Reich start for since he couldn't play in the game?

2. What was wrong with Jim Kelly?

3. True or False: This game still remains the greatest comeback in NFL history.

4. Who kicked the game winning field goal for the Bills in overtime?

5. True or False: The Oilers would get their revenge on the Bills several years later in the Playoffs.

6. True or False: Frank Reich would eventually return to Buffalo many years later.

7. True or False: The Bills and Oilers have a solid rivalry to this day.

8. Who leads the all-time Bills/Titans rivalry series?

9. Frank Reich also led one of the biggest comebacks ever when he played college football. Who did he play for and who did he beat?

10. How big was that deficit?

ANSWER

1. *Hall of Fame quarterback Jim Kelly.*
2. *He had a knee injury and didn't want to make it worse.*
3. *False. The Minnesota Vikings came back from being down 33-0 in 2022 to defeat the Indianapolis Colts 39-36.*
4. *Steve Christie.*
5. *True! The Oilers, who had become the Tennessee Titans, would beat the Bills in the 1999 Playoffs and advance to the Super Bowl.*
6. *True! Frank Reich eventually became the head coach of the Indianapolis Colts and lost to the Buffalo Bills in a playoff game.*
7. *True! Even though the team is no longer called the Houston Oilers, the Tennessee Titans and Buffalo Bills have played each other ever since 1960.*
8. *The Titans lead the series 30-20.*
9. *Frank Reich played for Maryland and led them to a comeback victory over Bernie Kosar and the Miami Hurricanes.*
10. *Maryland came back from being down 31-0 to beat Miami.*

"We definitely choked. We got outcoached, outplayed. There's no way we blow a 32-point lead with the talent we have. They made adjustments good enough to win the game. We didn't." -Cris Dishman.

"It's probably bigger in Buffalo than the Ice Bowl is in Green Bay or the Immaculate Reception is in Pittsburgh, because those cities have experienced eight Super Bowls between them. Since the Bills haven't won any, we kind of hang our hat on that comeback game ... In a way, it was our crowning moment." -Steve Tasker

"It reset the love affair with that team. People had become jaded, people had become upset with the idea that they just didn't see the success at the end of the rainbow. And now they had this, and this reminded them of how special this football team really is." -Vic Carruci

"I almost never, ever, ever give up, but at that point, I kind of did give up." -Barbara Beebe, mother of Bills wide receiver Don Beebe before the comeback happened.

"It was the biggest choke job in history ... I think we have to put another word in the English dictionary to describe this loss because devastated doesn't do it." -Cris Dishman

LESSONS FROM THE STORY

- Always be ready to go in sports or in life. Always have the next man up mentality, no matter what is going on.

- Nothing is over until it's over.

- Trust your teammates to make plays, and give them the confidence that you'll do the same thing for them.

- Never feel sorry for yourself.

- When an opportunity presents itself, take it!

19

DENVER BRONCOS

GALLOPING TOWARD GLORY WITH JOHN ELWAY

John Elway is now regarded as one of the greatest quarterbacks in NFL history. He stood 6'3" and weighed 215 pounds. He was absolutely fearless in the pocket when making throws downfield. And when he had to run, he could be incredibly hard to catch once he took off. But before 1997, he also had another label attached to his legacy: winless in the Super Bowl.

Elway and Denver made it to the big game three times in the 1980s—in 1986, 1987, and 1989—thanks to victories over the Cleveland Browns in the AFC Championship Game. But once the Broncos played under the bright lights for the Lombardi Trophy, they were absolutely demolished each and every time.

In Super Bowl 21, the Denver Broncos were hammered

39-20 by the New York Giants. The next year in Super Bowl 22, they were beaten even worse by Joe Gibbs and the Washington Redskins 42-10. And in Super Bowl 24, they were absolutely destroyed by Joe Montana and the San Francisco 49ers 55-10.

Denver would struggle to be competitive for the next several years following those bad losses. They made the playoffs in 1991, 1993, and 1996, but they were either upset by teams they shouldn't have lost to, or they had really bad seasons during the other years in the 1990s. But once 1997 rolled around, it was like Broncos owner Pat Bowlen and the rest of the team's leadership wanted a fresh start. And they took that quite literally. They ditched the classic logo and look they had been using since the team was founded in 1960. In its place was a dynamic, fast-looking new Bronco. A charging horse that looked like it was ready to take on anyone and everyone.

And in 1997, the Denver Broncos played just like that. They charged out of the starting gate, winning their first six games of the season. Five of them were blowout wins. John Elway was 37 years old by this point, but was still throwing the football as hard as he always had been. He had been the man in Denver for years, but many fans in the city and around the country thought this would be his last, and possibly best chance to win the Super Bowl before he was eventually forced to retire.

Thankfully for Elway, he wasn't the only one on this ride. He was backed by a solid supporting cast of other players that included running back Terrell Davis, veteran fullback Howard Griffith, wide receivers Ed McCaffrey and Rod Smith, and tight end Shannon Sharpe. The team also had a solid defense led by Neil Smith that was Top 10 in both yards and points allowed. They had all the pieces to make a run, but could they finally get the job done? In 1996, they arguably had a much more talented team, and that version of the Broncos was upset in the second round of the Playoffs by Jacksonville.

In 1997, the team came up against all the obstacles that every eventual champion goes through: overcoming inconsistency, doubting themselves, and struggling to keep the locker room together. And all these things would hit all at once when the team lost their Week 16 game against the San Francisco 49ers. By that point in the season, Denver had lost three of their last five games, including to the eventual AFC West Champion Kansas City Chiefs. But something even uglier happened after the Niners game. Something so potentially harmful to the chemistry of the team that the Broncos' leaders held a meeting behind closed doors after it happened.

After the Niners beat the Broncos, San Fran wide receiver JJ Stokes and Denver linebacker Bill Romanowski were nose to nose, with Stokes jawing at Romanowski. He was talking smack about the win. In an instant, Romanowski responded by spitting in Stokes' face. Before long, the incident was plastered all over every sports channel across the country. But the message coming out of Denver at that point was clear: the Broncos were at a tipping point. They were in danger of unraveling and falling apart at the worst possible time. If this kept up, they'd never even get back to the Super Bowl. Let alone win it!

In the team meeting, Bill Romanowski took responsibility for what he did. "What I did was wrong, and I apologized to them. When emotions are high, logic is low," he declared.

Tight end Shannon Sharpe was also outspoken about the situation: "I was upset at Romanowski not because he was white and spit in a black guy's face. But because he disrespected another man. And I couldn't condone what he did simply because he was my teammate. If my brother's wrong, he's wrong. I'm man enough to tell him he's wrong. And that's what I did. I was man enough to tell Bill Romanowski he was wrong."

After the team righted the ship and won their final game of the season against the Chargers to get to 12-4, the Broncos would then face three consecutive teams who had either beaten them that season, or broke their hearts the year before: Jacksonville, Kansas City, and Pittsburgh.

The Jaguars had gone into Mile High Stadium and knocked out a Super Bowl-caliber Broncos team in 1996 as a Wild Card. The Chiefs? They edged Denver earlier in 1997 and ended up taking the AFC West title by a single game. And Pittsburgh gave the Broncos a very rare ugly loss, as the Steelers smacked Denver 35-24.

The Broncos had learned their lesson. They ran the ball down Jacksonville's throat with Terrell Davis leading the way for a blowout 42-17 win. In Arrowhead Stadium the next week in Kansas City, Denver's defense shut down the Chiefs for a 14-10 win. In Pittsburgh, the defense once again finished the job, and the Broncos did something very, very few teams were able to do: beat the Steelers at Three Rivers Stadium. But they did just that. They won 24-21 to snag the AFC Championship trophy, and a date with the Packers in Super Bowl 32. For the first time since the end of the 1989 season, John Elway and his Broncos were headed back to the big dance!

However, everything was still stacked against Denver. John Elway was staring at a possible 0-4 Super Bowl record. They were 11-point underdogs to defending Super Bowl Champion Green Bay and Brett Favre in his prime. And everybody was ready to write the Broncos off before they even played the game. But Denver refused to roll over and die. They came after Brett Favre. The Broncos hit him hard and hit him often. They forced several turnovers. On the offensive side of the ball, it wasn't John Elway who had to be the hero. Instead, his team picked him up. Particularly Terrell Davis. Even though Davis was battling a migraine the whole game, #30 still shredded the Green Bay defense for 157 yards and three touchdowns. His three rushing touchdowns still stand as a Super Bowl record to this day.

After Denver's defense had sealed the game, the fireworks went off, and the confetti fell, Broncos owner Pat Bowlen didn't make a big victory speech. Instead, all Bowlen said was this: "There's one thing I want to say here tonight. And it's only four words: This one's for John."

After so many years of coming up short. After so many disappointing seasons. After so many close calls, John Elway could finally call himself a World Champion. And Denver finally had its first professional football title for the first time in 37 years.

"After 15 years of work, three Super Bowl losses, and all the different things that I'd gone through in my career, to finally reach the pinnacle of your sport and what you love to do, it's hard to explain," John Elway said. "I still get shivers when I think about it. I still get shivers because I can remember exactly how it felt. I had finally reached the pinnacle, and that's to be able to say that I was on a Super Bowl-winning team."

The next year, Denver would repeat as Super Bowl Champions, beating the Atlanta Falcons in Super Bowl 33. This gave Elway his second ring, and finally proved that the Broncos could win when it mattered most.

You will face obstacles in your life. You will come up short. It's part of growing up, and part of life itself. We can often learn more about ourselves from our losses in life than our wins.

Your losses do not define you. How you respond to them and move forward is what makes you who you are. Any failures you have in life do not define you either. How you respond to them is what makes you who you are. And once you power through, reaching victory becomes that much sweeter!

Take a cue from the 1997 Denver Broncos: Even if you've failed a bunch of times in the past. Don't give up. Champions don't quit!

- John Elway was born on June 28th, 1960.

- Played college football for Stanford.

- He was drafted by the Baltimore Colts first overall in the 1983 NFL Draft and soon traded to the Denver Broncos.

- Before John Elway led Denver on a magical run in 1997, he had never won the Super Bowl.

- John Elway set a franchise record in 1997 with 27 touchdown passes during the regular season.

- Jacksonville essentially mirrored Denver in how they played in both 1996 and 1997. The Jags beat the Broncos using their own playing style against them in 1996, while Denver learned their lesson and won in 1997.

- John Elway is now considered one of the greatest quarterbacks in NFL history because of how clutch he is. He made the biggest plays with the game on the line!

- Because of his clutch plays, John Elway was sometimes called "The Duke of Denver."

- He is a member of both the College Football Hall of Fame and the Pro Football Hall of Fame.

- The first time John Elway showed how clutch he could be was in the 1986 AFC Championship Game. In that game, he led the Denver Broncos on a 98-yard touchdown drive against the Cleveland Browns to tie the game in the final seconds. Denver would end up winning the game in overtime, and went to Super Bowl 21.

1. What number did John Elway wear throughout his career?

2. How many times did John Elway make it to the Pro Bowl?

3. How many game-winning drives did John Elway have in the playoffs?

4. True or False: John Elway was drafted by the New York Yankees for baseball, and almost played for them.

5. How many career touchdowns does John Elway have?

6. True or False: John Elway led the Broncos to back-to-back Super Bowl Championships in 1997 and 1998.

7. What was John Elway's career record in the Super Bowl?

8. Who did John Elway and the Broncos defeat to win their first Super Bowl?

9. True or False: John Elway also served as an executive for the Broncos.

10. True or False: Under his as GM and Executive VP, the Broncos won a Super Bowl.

ANSWER

1. #7.
2. nine times.
3. 6
4. True!
5. He has exactly 300 passing touchdowns.
6. True!
7. 2-3.
8. The Green Bay Packers.
9. True! He was the team's General Manager, and Executive Vice President of Football Operations from 2011-2023.
10. True! They won Super Bowl 50.

"I've experienced the highest of highs and lowest of lows. I think to really appreciate anything you have to be at both ends of the spectrum."

"If you ask what's been my secret of success, most might say it's my God-given athletic ability to throw a football. While talent is important, it's not necessarily the most important thing. Thousands of talented people fail every day. My strength has been my will to win-that competitive fire inside."

"I always believe there's a reason why you go through everything."

"I look at my career and it's still hard for me to believe the way things turned out and how things happened. I've been so blessed."

"I was so lucky to walk away with two Super Bowls and know that the last year was positive."

LESSONS FROM THE STORY

• If at first you don't succeed, keep trying!

• It takes guts to stick around, and turn a bad situation into a good one.

• Keep your emotions in check and stay focused on whatever it is you're doing. If you lose your cool, bad things can happen.

• Don't just take the credit for when you do well, take responsibility for when you fail.

• Any obstacle can be overcome if you work hard enough, and want your dream badly enough.

20

JERRY RICE

THE GOAT OF WIDE RECEIVERS!

It does not matter if someone is a seasoned football fan who has followed the game for decades, or if they're a young fan still learning about the sport. When the name of Jerry Rice is mentioned in football conversation, most fans imagine a tall and long wide receiver who made all kinds of circus catches, and won several Super Bowls. But what if I told you that Jerry Rice becoming the greatest wide receiver in NFL history almost never happened?

Jerry Rice grew up in tiny Crawford, Mississippi, a town of 600 people. He was the sixth of eight children. Jerry's father, Joe was a man's man. He was big and strong and worked as a bricklayer. He often brought Jerry and his brothers along to help with jobs when they were growing up. They all laid bricks and built houses for others. But even though Jerry's mind wasn't on football this early in his life, he instinctively knew he was meant for something more, even though bricklaying instilled good character in young Jerry and taught him the value of hard work.

Bricklaying with his dad Joe may have laid the foundations of Jerry's character. But the first thing that really set his destiny in motion was actually from something bad. He got in trouble for playing hooky from school. The school principal spotted Jerry and a friend cutting class, which freaked Jerry out and made him run off. But instead of punishing him, the principal was surprised at Jerry's speed, and let the high school football coach know about him. The coach immediately offered Jerry a spot on the team.

Up until that point, Jerry had never really played football in high school. Sure, he played pickup games with his friends in the neighborhood. But high school was the first time he really showed off glimpses of who he would eventually become. Even though Jerry had never played organized football up until that point, something also changed in him once he suited up for Moor High School: he locked in. He found what his purpose was in life and didn't let go. He was as stubborn as a bulldog.

His mother initially fought him on it. She didn't want him playing football, as she feared it was too rough for him. But his stubbornness won her over. And it was this stubbornness that would be one of his defining characteristics later in his career.

Jerry played several different positions when he was younger, including defensive back, tight end, and running back. But where he really flourished was at wide receiver. Rice was eventually contacted by over 40 different big-time schools, but not one of them offered him a scholarship. So he went to Mississippi Valley State to play for Archie Cooley. In today's college football world, many college prospects choose which school to play for based on their position coaches. But when Jerry Rice played college football for the Delta Devils, their entire offensive game plan was based on the passing game. They threw the football so much that Coach Cooley was even nicknamed "Gunslinger."

Under Cooley and with talented quarterback Willie Totten throwing him the football, Rice got progressively better until he had record-shattering junior and senior seasons! In 1983, as a junior, Rice hauled in 102 catches for 1,450 receiving yards, which led the NCAA. He was even better as a senior, snagging 112 catches for 1,845 yards and 27 touchdowns, which was a national record for any division of NCAA football!

Needless to say, this grabbed the attention of San Francisco head coach Bill Walsh, and the Niners traded up to 16th overall in the 1985 draft and took Rice just before Dallas had a chance to get him. For the next 16 seasons, Jerry Rice would thrill the Bay Area with clutch catch after clutch catch. He'd stuff the stat sheet with several 100-yard and even 200-yard receiving performances. But one thing remained the same throughout his time with the Niners: his work ethic.

Early on, his teammates and other players would poke fun at Jerry because he was often concerned with how he looked. But when it came time to either prepare for a game, or execute during gametime, nobody would outwork #80. It didn't matter if it was Joe Montana or Steve Young throwing the football to him, Jerry Rice was the receiver who often made the whole system work well for Bill Walsh and the Niners. Whether he outran opposing defenses to catch deep bombs, or he made defenders miss on short pass plays to turn them into long gains. And this didn't change whether it was in the regular season or the Playoffs. Rice often came up clutch when his team needed him the most. Perhaps his biggest game that he ever played in, was Super Bowl 23 against the Cincinnati Bengals on January 22, 1989.

On that night, Rice exploded. He snagged 11 catches for 215 yards and three touchdowns against a Bengals defense that was otherwise pretty solid. And even though he didn't catch the game-winning touchdown in that Super Bowl victory, Rice was the key player on the game-winning drive, and kept the Niners moving down the field until they took home a Championship!

Rice won two more rings with the Niners in Super Bowl 24 and Super Bowl 29 before the team decided to go in a different direction with a younger wide receiver in Terrell Owens. Not to mention the Niners were also in full rebuilding mode by the time they released Rice. But Jerry surprisingly didn't slow down or lose a step once he became an Oakland Raider in 2001. In fact, he was one of the Raiders' biggest weapons, along with Tim Brown, another veteran wide receiver.

Jerry Rice finally hung up his cleats for good in 2006, But his record speaks for itself, especially during his time in San Francisco. Here's how big of a mark Jerry Rice made on the NFL and the game of football:

- Hall of Famer (Class of 2010)
- Three-time Super Bowl Champion.
- Thirteen-time Pro Bowler
- Two-time Offensive Player of the Year
- Six-time NFL receiving yards leader.
- Two-time NFL receptions leader.
- Six-time NFL receptions leader.

That kind of resume speaks for itself. Jerry Rice isn't just one of the greatest receivers to play in the NFL, he's one of the greatest players overall. And the biggest reason for this, is he went the extra mile. He worked harder than most people. Whether it was involuntary team workouts during the season, extra route running during practice and before and after games, or simply working out six hours a day during the offseason, Jerry Rice worked harder than most of his teammates and competitors.

The humble son of a bricklayer is now a Pro Football Hall of Famer and the greatest wide receiver in the game. Jerry struggled growing up when money was tight, and when it was just him, his parents and seven other siblings. But once he found his purpose and what he was good at, he took his dream and ran with it, and worked as hard as he could to make that dream a reality!

You have a chance to do the same in your life. But first, find that thing that you're not only good at, make sure it's something that gets you out of bed in the morning. A lot of people don't like hard work. It hurts either mentally, physically or both. But if you have something that you're truly passionate about and excited to pursue as you grow up, it should be a lot easier for you to go after your dream if you love it that much. Maybe your dream is to be an athlete or football player like Jerry Rice was. Or maybe your dream is to be a doctor, lawyer, scientist, or any other great career.

If you have that spark, passion for it, and the desire to pursue the dream no matter what it takes to realize it, that's the same passion that Jerry Rice had for his career. And all that passion and dedication made him the greatest wide receiver in NFL history!

If you pursue your dreams in that way and with that level of dedication, maybe you'll become the doctor who cures cancer, a great future President of the United States, or the first person on Mars. But passion combined with dedication opens up limitless possibilities. How far you go is only limited by your imagination. Jerry Rice proved that in his career!

- He would often look up Michael Irvin's stats to keep up with him. Michael Irvin was a Hall of Fame wide receiver with the Cowboys who was similar to Jerry Rice in terms of skill level. They were both big-time playmakers!

- He finished ninth in the Heisman Trophy voting as a senior at Mississippi Valley State. He was greatly overlooked in college, probably because MVSU was a NCAA 1-AA football team. This means that Mississippi Valley State is a much smaller school than normal college football teams.

- When Jerry Rice retired, he signed a one-day contract from the 49ers totaling $1,985,806.49. This was symbolic, and he didn't receive any money. But the numbers stood for the year he was drafted (1985), his jersey number (80), the year he retired (06) and the team that drafted him (49 for 49ers).

- Hall of Famer (Class of 2010)

- Three-time Super Bowl Champion.

- 13-time Pro Bowler

- Two-time Offensive Player of the Year

- Six-time NFL receiving yards leader.

- Two-time NFL receptions leader.

- Six-time NFL receptions leader.

1. How many career catches did Jerry Rice have?

2. How many receiving yards does Jerry Rice have?

3. How many career receiving touchdowns does Jerry Rice have?

4. What number did Jerry Rice wear?

5. Why did he wear that number?

6. What was Jerry Rice's nickname when he played football?

7. True or False: Jerry Rice only ever played for the San Francisco 49ers.

8. Which teams did Jerry Rice play for?

9. True or False: He is a member of both the College Football Hall of Fame and the Pro Football Hall of Fame.

10. When was Jerry Rice inducted into the Pro Football Hall of Fame?

ANSWER

1. *1,549 catches, an NFL record.*
2. *22,895 career receiving yards, also an NFL record.*
3. *197 receiving touchdowns, another NFL record.*
4. *He most famously wore #80.*
5. *He wanted to pay tribute to his idol, former Seahawks wide receiver and Hall of Famer, Steve Largent.*
6. *"World." Rice earned that nickname because of his world-class talent, and because he could catch almost anything that was thrown his way.*
7. *False. He wanted to finish his career there, but ended up playing for three other teams.*
8. *The San Francisco 49ers, Oakland Raiders, Seattle Seahawks and Denver Broncos.*
9. *True!*
10. *2010*

"Today I will do what others won't, so tomorrow I can accomplish what others can't."

"The Enemy of the best is the good. If you're always settling with what's good, you'll never be the best."

"I think my secret is that there's no shortcuts for hard work, determination and having that don't give up attitude."

"I think the thing about that was I was always willing to work; I was not the fastest or biggest player but I was determined to be the best football player I could be on the football field and I think I was able to accomplish that through hard work."

"You know, I never looked down the road and said, 'Hey look, one day, the Hall of Fame.' It's always about playing each and every game 100 percent and I thank my teammates for getting me into the Hall because football is a team sport, not an individual sport."

LESSONS FROM THE STORY

- If you want to be great, there's no substitute for hard work.

- Once you find your purpose in life, whether you're younger or older, go after it!

- Sometimes people might overlook you. That's okay. Don't worry about them. Just continue working hard to get where you need to be.

- Work ethic beats talent. Every single time.

- The most successful people in anything, always work harder than everybody else.

REFERENCES

10 Facts You Didn't Know about Baker Mayfield-NFL Therapy

10 Things You Didn't Know about CJ Stroud-YouTube

12 Facts: Doug Flutie-ESPN Honolulu

1997 Denver Broncos season-Wikipedia

20 Things You Probably Didn't Know about Tom Brady-Business Insider

2009 New Orleans Saints season-Wikipedia

25 Things You Didn't Know about Jerry Rice-Complex

A Football Life Derrick Thomas-YouTube

A Football Life Doug Flutie-YouTube

A look back at the life of Gale Sayers, his friendship with Brian Piccolo through the eyes of the Pi-YouTube

A Super Season. Part I: How the 1997 Broncos were fueled by a gut-wrenching playoff loss to the Jaguars-Denver Broncos

American Underdog-Wikipedia

America's Game 1997 Denver Broncos-YouTube

Andre Reed on comebacks: The game, and 2015 Bills-YouTube

AP Story: Favre's Father Dies At 58-Packers

Baker Mayfield-It doesn't matter what cards you're…Brainy Quote

Becoming the Goat: The Tom Brady Story | Free Documentary | Full HD |Documentary Central-YouTube

Biggest comeback in NFL history: Re-visiting Bills vs. Oilers-Sports Illustrated

Bill Russell and Kareem Abdul Jabbar at the Famous Cleveland Summit with Muhammad Ali-YouTube

Bob Stoops and Baker Mayfield on their very first conversation | Conversations with Coach-YouTube

Brett Favre: Biography, NFL Hall of Fame QB, Welfare Scandal-Biography

Brian Piccolo's daughter remembers Gale Sayers-The Washington Post

Browns reliable tackle Joe Thomas finally gets biggest victory, enshrinement into Hall of Fame-AP News

Browns: Baker Mayfield gets brutally honest on confusing Cleveland exit-Clutch Points

CJ Stroud: 3 little known facts about the Texans quarterback-Clutch Points

CJ Stroud: A Story of Adversity, Faith, and Forgiveness-YouTube

Cleveland honors athletes, activists involved in 1967 summit-YouTube

Cleveland Summit-Wikipedia

Derrick Thomas Quiz | NFL Players | 10 Questions-Fun Trivia

Derrick Thomas-Wikipedia

Doug Flutie College Debut at QB-10/10/81-YouTube

Brian's life a Song of friendship, courage-ESPN Classic

ESPN Special on Vince Papale-YouTube

"Favre's Dad Game" | Brett Gives it All for Big Irv | A Football Life | NFL Films-YouTube

Full Interview: Jerry Rice-YouTube

Garrett Hartley Talks About Feel of Winning Kick-YouTube

How Joe Thomas helped carry the Browns and played his way to the Pro Football Hall of Fame-NFL.com

How This Homeless Man Became an NFL Star-YouTube

Jake Plummer Talks About Pat Tillman Being the Greatest Person-YouTube

Jerry Rice-Stats, Retirement & Facts-Biography

Jim Brown talks about his friendship with Muhammad Ali | NFL-YouTube

Joe Thomas' Incredible Journey to the Hall of Fame-YouTube

Kurt Warner: Biography, Career, Net Worth, Family, Top Stories for the Hall of Fame QB-Sportscasting

Kurt Warner-Wikipedia

Lions vs. Rams postgame locker room celebration-YouTube

Michael Irvin Facts for Kids-Kiddle

Michael Irvin Gets Emotional with Warren Sapp about His Dad Passing Away When He was 17 (Part 3)-YouTube

Michael Irvin Impassioned Hall of Fame Speech | NFL Network-YouTube

Michael Irvin reflects on winning the Super Bowl in 1993 | First Take-YouTube

Mike Ditka Doubles Down on Walter Payton Bears Super Bowl Regret-Outkick

New Lions head coach Dan Campbell: 'We're going to bite a kneecap off'-YouTube

NFL All-Time Team: Favre on what drove him to play on 'MNF' after his dad died-YouTube

Packers 41-7 Raiders (Dec 22, 2003) Game Recap-ESPN

Pat Tillman: In His Own Words-YouTube

Pat Tillman-Biography, NFL Football Player, Military-Biography

Pat's Story-Pat Tillman Foundation

Raiders rookie Josh Jacobs buys his father a new house | Exclusive ESPN Interview | SportsCente-YouTube

Speech from "Brian's Song"-YouTube

Super Bowl XLIV: Saints vs. Colts highlights-YouTube

Super Bowl XXXIV Recap: Rams vs. Titans | NFL-YouTube

The Chicago Bears: 5 Facts You Might Not Know about Walter Payton (Blog)-Agate Publishing

The Comeback (American football)-Wikipedia

The Greatest Comeback Ever Happened 31 Years Ago in Buffalo-Wyrk

The Greatest Show on Turf: Legacy of the 1999-2001 St. Louis Rams | The Timeline-YouTube

The Life and Career of Doug Flutie (Complete Story)-Pro Football History

The Life and Career of WR Michael Irvin (Complete Story)-Pro Football History

The Tillman Story-YouTube

The Unembellished Story of Vince Papale | News, Scores, Highlights, Stats, and Rumors-Bleacher Report

Through Hell & Back: The Dark Backstory of CJ Stroud-YouTube

Tom Brady Stats, Height, Weight, Position, Draft, College-Pro Football Reference

Walter Payton Pranks with the 1985 Chicago Bears-YouTube

Walter Payton's Legendary Prank on Ron Rivera | Rookie Handbook | NFL Now-YouTube

What Happened to Vince Papale From Invincible? (His Real Football Story Vs the Movie)-YouTube